TENACIOUS
HOPE

Discovering

JOY AND PEACE

in God's Perfect Plan

Bridging THE *Gap*

CONTENTS

Section 3: Tenacious Hope Inspires Me To...

$\mathscr{J}NTRODUCTION$

"There is no greater love than to lay down one's life for one's friends."
John 15:13 (NLT)

Hope is a gift, but tenacious hope is feisty! What exactly is *tenacious hope?*

According to Hebrew and Greek translations, *hope* is an indicator of certainty. "Hope" signifies "a strong and confident expectation." It is the confident certainty that what God has promised is true. In the Bible, hope is never a static or passive expression. It is dynamic, active, creative, life-sustaining, and tenacious!

Here are a some of my favorite ways to think about hope:

- Hope is not an escape from reality or our problems. Instead, it pushes us to get moving!
- Hope changes how we view ourselves, helping us to recognize that we're on a journey.
- Hope changes what we value as we become Heaven-minded.
- Hope spurs us to reconsider the choices we make with our time, treasure, and talent.

"Tenacious" means keeping a firm hold of something, clinging closely and not readily relinquishing a course of action.

In my mind, someone who embodies this is my friend, fellow kingdom-worker and Christ-follower Linda Miller.

Linda has fought a tenacious battle with cancer for almost 10 years. As I spent time with her over the last few months, Linda would often tell me, "I will never lose hope, because I know God heals and performs miracles. However, as I am about to depart from this life to the next—while I believe in miracles more than ever—I know that my hope is in my relationship with Jesus. He is so personal and real!"

Just last week as I sat with Linda, she said to me, "I'm hoping for a few more days. I would like to go to the cabin for a long weekend with my family. After, I'd like to host a tea party for my 11-year-old granddaughter. Then if I'm still here, I am going to take my two oldest granddaughters to the Mall of America for a shopping weekend. I told my hubby, 'I think I might need a fair amount of cash!'"

I told her that she amazed me, and she replied, "I told one of my nurses a while back, 'I don't know how to die; I've never done that before!'"

The nurse responded with encouragement, "None of us have, but let me tell you this: As you are preparing for your departure, the most important thing you can do is to keep living life! By doing so, you are not only teaching your family, children, and grandchildren how to live but also how to die."

We continued to pray, chat, smile, laugh, and enjoy being together that day.

I'd like to dedicate this devotional to Linda for always looking at life through the lens of hope. You're my hero.

Carol Lund

Director, Bridging the Gap

SECTION 1

TENACIOUS HOPE

Is Anchored In...

1

Tenacious Hope is Anchored In the Storm

SUSIE LARSON

"As evening came, Jesus said to his disciples,
'Let's cross to the other side of the lake.'"

Mark 4:35 (ESV)

It had been a full, fruitful day of ministry. The day drew to a close, the sky darkened, and Jesus pointed to the water. He urged his disciples to get into the boat and cross to the other side. They pushed away from shore, sailed for a bit. Then, a mega storm hit. The winds raged, the waves surged, and the disciples feared for their lives.

Have you been there?

You followed Jesus, and he led you right into a storm?

What happened next? Did you doubt God's love? Wonder about his plan? Fear you heard him wrong?

You're not alone.

The disciples followed Jesus into the center of brutal a storm that could have killed them. Afraid, disoriented, and dismayed, they asked, "Jesus, don't you care?"

Imagine their swirling thoughts. *Jesus, we've left everything to follow you. We're going to die tonight and you're sleeping. In this storm! If you were all-knowing, you'd know how bad things are. You wouldn't be sleeping soundly in the chaos. What were you thinking, bringing us out here?*

Maybe you feel the same. You wonder if Jesus somehow messed up your itinerary and you're left with the mess. You're hurt, disoriented, and dismayed. How could this have happened? Where are you, Lord?

Jesus was out cold. The disciples literally had to wake him up.

Then he rose up, and spoke to the storm.

Suddenly, all was peaceful again.

Prior to this epic moment, the rains raged, the winds screamed, the boat started to sink. Knowing what they'd just been through, Jesus asked his disciples, "Why are you afraid? Do you still have no faith?"

Given the circumstances, doesn't it make sense that they were afraid?

The disciples couldn't know that a new level of ministry awaited them on the other side of the lake. But Jesus knew. He loved these men. He knew they needed to know how to hold onto peace in the midst of chaos. They needed to know how to rest when they were tempted to live stressed. And, they needed to know how to activate their faith, use their authority, and find their footing when the elements rage against them.

He's a good Shepherd and he leads us into seasons and storms and situations that test and try our faith, that refine our character, and that prepare us for the road up ahead.

We don't know what ministry opportunities he's prepared for us. We don't know what enemy schemes await us. We can't fathom the storms that may confront us.

But what we do know is that we're equipped. For all of it.

Every promise of God is ours in Christ Jesus.

Every word of the Lord is true.

Everything that comes against us, God can purpose for us.

Every tear, he collects.

Every trial, he uses.

Every hurt, he will heal.

And in every storm, he'll reveal his power to us.

Jesus told his disciples, and he tells us, this important truth:

"Look, I have given you authority over all the power of the enemy, and you can walk among snakes and scorpions and crush them. Nothing will injure you," (Luke 10:19).

He's given us authority. Now it's time to take authority.

Speak perfect love to your fears.

Speak peace to your storms.

Speak life to a world in need.

Storms won't last forever. Seasons will most certainly change.

But Jesus's love and his presence in your life will never change. If he leads you to it, he'll lead you through it. He's attentive to every need and he's always good. You have him, you have his promises, and you're stronger than you know. You're going to be okay. Fight for a right perspective. Jesus will use every moment in your life to conform you to his image and to prepare you for a fruitful, future ministry.

Hold onto hope. Keep the faith. Tenaciously trust him. He is worthy of it all.

Reflect and Respond

What are the blessings in your current battles? Can you see Jesus at work here?

_____

_____

_____

Hebrews 12:12 tells us to take a new grip with our tired hands and to strengthen our weak knees. Are you willing to do that today?

_____

_____

_____

Susie Larson is a national speaker, radio host, and author of 15 books. She's a wife, mother, and grandma to one adorable grandson.

2

Tenacious Hope Is Anchored In
His Wings

JEN SPIEGEL

"Hope is a thing with feathers that perches in the soul,
And sings the tune without the words
And never stops at all."

—*Emily Dickinson*

It was a chilly October evening when a little surprise, in the form of a stray cat, showed up on our back deck. Two little eyes, the color of Egyptian gold, beamed in at us as we ate dinner. Following a chorus of, "Can we feed it?," and, "Mom, look how sad it is out there in the cold," of course, I caved. After inhaling a hot dog gleefully provided by my children, the skinny orange fur ball settled on top of a small pile of leaves just outside the patio door. And there it stayed, mewing its expectant song like a birdie on a perch, seeming to sense my crumbling resolve.

Darkness descended, and still the cat remained. Despite my husband's allergy to cats, and the fact that we certainly weren't in the market for another pet, I couldn't quite get myself to close the curtains in its face. Just as big of a softie as I am when it comes to animals, my husband eventually said, "Alright, bring it in for a little while."

"You know what's going to happen if that thing comes in the house, right?" I asked.

He nodded and sighed.

We were doomed.

It didn't take long for our little houseguest to make herself at home. And over the next few weeks, she wiggled her way right into our hearts.

It was the middle of November when I noticed something strange about the cat. As she strolled over to me one day for a snuggle, the once thin-as-a-rail cat seemed a little . . . fat. And over the next few days, as her stomach seemed to expand more and more, it hit me.

This cat was pregnant.

While part of me questioned the wisdom of raising a litter of kittens in our already full house, a bigger part of me was nearly bursting with excitement. *This!* I told myself. *This has to be why this straggler showed up at our house. She needs a safe place to bring new life into the world!*

Who could argue with that reasoning? Although my itchy-eyed, sneezing husband and I had already come to an agreement that the cat simply couldn't stay, I convinced him to hold off on finding a new home for the cat until the kittens were ready to go to homes of their own.

My excitement grew as the weeks passed and the cat continued to expand. I eagerly counted the days until what Google and I had estimated was her due date. I researched how to care for kittens and crafted a birthing hut from a cardboard box and old towels. I planned the pictures I would take of the kittens tangled up with ribbons under the Christmas tree. Just as Google told me to do, I increased the cat's food supply to meet her voracious appetite.

We were ready. And yet, it seemed the cat wasn't.

Her due date, and a few adjusted due dates, passed uneventfully. Each morning I ran downstairs to see if, perhaps, finally the kittens had made their debut. But each morning I was disappointed.

Finally, just before Christmas, I couldn't wait any longer. I made an appointment with the vet and lugged the overdue mama into the pet hospital.

After examining the cat's belly for a few moments, the vet looked up at me with the hint of a smile.

"Well, it looks like this cat isn't pregnant. She's just . . . fat."

I'm sure my eyes nearly bugged out of my head. *Just FAT?*

"You'll want to decrease her food consumption by at least 30 percent."

Mortified, I mumbled my thanks, tucked Fat Cat under my arm, and booked it out of there as quickly as possible, hope deflating like an untied balloon.

Later that evening, I broke down the birthing hut, folded the unused towels, and placed an online ad for a sweet, silly, and just plain fat cat. As I worked, I thought about the hope I'd felt, the excitement at the possibility of new life, and how in an instant it had all seemed to deflate.

What, I wondered, *is the point of hope when so often it doesn't seem to influence the outcome?*

Sometimes it's a little thing, like the misinterpretation of a few extra pounds on a hungry houseguest.

But sometimes it's big. And watching our dreams slip away can be so painful.

Sometimes hoping for a certain ending feels like a fool's game.

Within hours of placing the ad, adoption inquiries started pouring in. Two days after the embarrassing appointment with the vet, I watched as our unexpected visitor turned her golden eyes toward the face of her new owners, then gently dipped her head to meet their eager hands. A few minutes later, they drove away without a backward glance, fully engrossed in their new little family.

I expected to feel a little sad saying goodbye. Instead, my heart felt featherlight. And I realized something.

Hope is more than circumstances, more than a satisfying conclusion.

Hope is a home.

Psalm 91:4 explains it like this: *"He will cover you with his feathers, and under his wings you will find refuge."*

We have a home that will outlast every surprise, every heartbreak, every step of our journey. And the door is always open.

I may not know what's to come of the many things I hope for. But I do know a big feathery Father who has set his very self over me. I know a Savior with an eager hand stretched out, inviting a blue-eyed straggler like me to settle in, like a birdie on a perch, and join in a song that rises and falls, one moment a crescendo, the next so quiet I must be completely still to hear it.

So I sing—as loud as I can—three words I know to be true above all others:

This is home.

Reflect and Respond

What are your favorite things about home?

_____

_____

_____

What does it mean to make a home under God's wings?

_____

_____

_____

Recall a time you hoped for something that didn't turn out as you expected. How can you begin to reframe that experience in light of your eternal home?

_____

_____

_____

Jen Spiegel is an advisor and editor for Bridging the Gap's writing team, where she shares her passion for honest storytelling and helping women discover the healing power of writing. She enjoys date nights, outdoor adventures with her family, and curling up with a good book and a one-eyed dog named Finn. You can connect with her at storiesinthetrees.com.

3

Tenacious Hope Is Anchored In God's Purpose for Me

HEATHER GILMORE

"And we know that in all things God works for the good of those who love him, who have been called according to his purpose."

Romans 8:28 (NIV)

Two years ago, I was diagnosed with a mental illness that stems from the core belief that I am worthless, along with dual fears of abandonment and rejection instilled in me during very traumatic formative years.

Yet my unshakable faith in God doesn't lessen my struggle. In fact, it *adds* to it. How can I be worthless, when God created me and says otherwise? This kind of push-and-pull inside me is a daily fight.

The other day, I had an emotional breakdown. I confessed to my roommates that I felt like a failure. I finally had to face and accept my limitations: I cannot hold down a steady job like the rest of them. To be honest, this truth often makes me feel as though my future holds no hope.

I asked aloud, "How can I be worth something if I can't maintain a normal lifestyle?"

Before anyone could speak, the internal answer I heard was immediate. The spirit of the Lord replied, "Because you were made to be *extraordinary*."

Romans 8:28 says, "And we know that in all things God works for the good of those who love him, who have been called according to his purpose" (NIV).

When we read this verse, so often we get caught by the first part. But what about the rest of the verse?

"...who have been called according to his purpose."

What if your purpose in this life is *not* to be like everyone else? We're often so narrowly focused on the school-job-marriage-home formula of life that we miss out on what God has for us. We lose hope in our futures.

Man's purpose is formulaic. God's is box-breaking, world-changing, earth-shattering. I have to wonder if half of my anxiety comes from just trying to fit myself into a box that was never meant for me. It's no wonder I feel hopeless.

But feelings are not facts. I may feel hopeless, but that does not mean I have no hope. Just the opposite—I have all the hope in the universe at my beck and call!

I've found that renewing my hope requires me to shift toward God. I need to begin to ask what his purpose is for me. I need to let go of my own expectations, my expectations of others, and my fears about my needs. I cannot cling to hope when my hands are filled with other things.

I remind myself often that God has never let me down. When I focus on his promise—that I have been called according to his purpose and can trust him to help me see it through—I know that nothing is impossible.

We often don't understand the path God has us on. We see the lives of those around us and wonder why our own lives don't look like theirs. We wonder if we're doing something wrong, how we've failed, or what we could do differently. We give in to fears and anxieties we were never meant to bear.

Comparing ourselves can often leave us feeling like we're failing, when in fact we may be right where God wants us to be.

Let go of the fears you cling to, and grab hold of the hope God offers. Spend time with him, and ask him what his purpose is for you. The path you are on is one only you can walk, fashioned especially for your feet.

You are meant for an extraordinary life, filled with the blessings only God could give. It isn't easy, I know. I'm right there with you in the struggle. But that's one more promise: we are never alone. And there is so much hope, even in that.

We are extraordinary beings, offered an even more extraordinary hope.

Reflect and Respond

What fears or anxieties are you holding on to?

_____

_____

_____

Are you prepared to surrender those fears so that you can begin to receive the hope of the extraordinary life he has purposed for you? What, if anything, is holding you back?

_____

_____

_____

Heather Gilmore is a writer, nerd, and all-around silly person. She loves Minnesota, people, hugs, books, and board games. Her friends have become her family, and, although she's not perfect at it, she's made it a life goal to ensure everyone she meets knows that they are deeply and truly loved.

4

Tenacious Hope Is Anchored In
His Image

PATNACIA GOODMAN

"So God created [humankind] in His own image,
in the image and likeness of God He created him;
male and female He created them."

Genesis 1:27 (AMP)

So I have this mug. While I prefer my coffee iced, a warm morning brew has become part of my daily routine, so a good mug is a necessity. It has to be deep enough to hold the right amount of liquid gold, wide enough to wrap a hand around, and also have a handle that doesn't cause finger cramps.

Anyway, back to this mug. I bought it for its size (14 ounces of coffee; yes, please!), and liked its simplicity: off-white with a singular word etched in thin, black letters:

Hope.

Even though I was familiar with the word, I realized I didn't really know what hope meant or how it applied to my life. So one morning, I poured a cup of coffee into my mug and sat down to study this small but spunky word. Little did I know, a year after buying that mug, how much that word would grow on me as I grew in my understanding of it.

The power of hope can't be overstated. Often paired with faith, which is powerful and intentional belief, I see hope as the energizing current, the anticipation that the things we believe for are coming (Hebrews 11:1). In that way, hope fuels faith.

Well then, what fuels hope?

I believe that our hope as believers is fueled by and rooted in the growth of our relationships with God. It is one thing to know him and who he says he is. It's another, deeper thing to become women so rooted in that truth that we become filled with steady confidence in his ability above our shortcomings and life's impossibilities.

And to truly be women of hope, we need to know who the one we put our hope in says we are.

You see, when our hope is anchored in a right and firm understanding of our purpose and place in Christ, it springs eternally. That hope isn't swayed by delay, nor is it easily stripped away by disappointment.

In fact, it's hard to lose hope when we grow more and more aware of the hands that knit us together with love and absolute care. More often than I'd like to admit, I forget what God said in Genesis 1. After creating everything we can see—every bird and flower and star—with nothing but the power of his voice, he says, "Let us make human beings in our image, to be like us" (1:26, NLT). And then he did just that.

My friends, we were created from the will of the Almighty God, who desired fellowship with beings who were like him. Paul says it well when he calls us God's *poiema*—his workmanship, his masterpiece—created in Christ—our brother, savior and king—for purposeful works that he planned for us long before we existed on this earth (Ephesians 2:10).

These beautiful pictures of how much God values us make hope flourish within me. Throughout the Word of God we find more names and more descriptions of who we are, definitions that hold firm when doubts try to erode the hope I've built up within.

When I look at my body with shame, I find hope in the fact that he calls me a temple, a dwelling place for his Spirit (1 Cor. 6:19-20).

When I feel isolated and lonely, I find hope and courage to reach out, because he has called me to be part of his Body (1 Cor. 12:27).

And when unworthiness creeps in, hope swells within me because he calls me loved, so loved that he sacrificed his own son to secure my adoption (John 3:16, Gal. 4:4-5).

To be known and named by the Creator of the Universe! I can't help but quote the psalmist who says, "Such knowledge is too wonderful for me." Every day that I root myself in the truth of who I am, I can't help but be infused with hope.

Hope that says the sting of today's circumstances pale in comparison to the life the Maker of Heaven and Earth has planned for us.

Hope that whispers, *Be still and seek Him. He will be there, when chaos is all around.*

Hope that shouts that I am a daughter of the King of kings, the Father of fathers, when the enemy tries to convince me I am anything but.

So sisters, I pray we anchor our hope in that truth—that we are who he says we are: his image-bearers, daughters of the King.

Reflect and Respond

In your own words, how is hope connected to identity?

_____

_____

_____

What areas of your identity need to be infused with hope? Write down three areas, then search the Bible for what it says about who you really are.

_____

_____

_____

Patnacia Goodman is a story-loving, winter-loathing Minnesota native. As the acquisitions associate for Bethany House Publishers, she is living her high school dreams, helping books come to life. She also loves playing board games, recommending TV shows, and occasionally updating her personal blog. For more musings and ramblings, find her at patnacia.wordpress.com or on Instagram and Twitter @patnaciag.

5

Tenacious Hope is Anchored In
God's Truth

NANCY HOLTE

"My heart is confident in you, O God; my heart is confident.
No wonder I can sing your praises!"

Psalm 57:7 (NLT)

When my husband, John, was diagnosed with cancer five years ago, I was a basket case. There were lots of tears, fear, and times when I wondered if I'd have to finish out my life alone. But then, I grabbed hold of hope—a confident hope that John would be healed. In my "perfect world" mind, I was praying for a miraculous healing that would eliminate all the chemo, trips to the Mayo clinic, and the ensuing stem-cell transplant. But that didn't happen.

At that same time—during his first few months of treatment—a local magazine decided to write an article on John and his experience. I remember sitting with the interviewer and confidently stating that God would heal my husband. I believe what the Bible says about healing: "'But He was pierced for our transgressions, He was crushed for our iniquities; the punishment that brought us peace was upon Him, and *by His wounds we are healed,*" Isaiah 53:5 (NIV). Tenacious hope is a hope rooted in God's word. It's a hope that says, "I believe God is going to do what he said he would." That's why I believed my husband would be healed, and I said as much to the interviewer.

I read once that instead of asking God over and over again for the same thing, we should ask him once and then thank him, from there on out, for the answer to our prayers. So that's what I did. Every night, I prayed, "Thank you, God, that John is healed." Because when God promises something in his word, and we ask according to that promise, we can know that he will answer. His answer may not look the way we want it to, but he will answer.

But what we also told the interviewer is that our faith was, and is, not based on whether or not God would heal John the way we believed he would. Our faith is based on knowing that God is a good God and always has our best in mind. Had God's best for John been that he be healed in heaven, I was ready for that answer. I know plenty of people who are filled with faith who pray for their loved one to be healed, and they aren't. I would never say that their family member wasn't healed because they lacked enough faith or hope. That's not how God works. It's not a contest of how much faith we have, or how many people we can rally to pray for us (although I would never hesitate to ask for as many prayers as possible). It's a matter of trusting that God is for you, regardless of the outcome.

There were times, of course, when my tenacious hope wavered. I remember, at Christmas that year, how John helped me set up our Christmas tree. We were in the middle of the "Is it straight?" routine when I burst into tears. My sweet husband probably thought I was overreacting to a tipping tree, but then I said, "You can't die! I can't do this alone!" John just looked at me and said, "I'm not planning on dying."

I'm happy to say that John is now in remission. However, doctors say his cancer is treatable, not curable. Every four months we drive back to the Mayo Clinic for tests to see where he's at with his numbers. To be honest, this isn't the solution I was hoping for. Like I said, I wanted a "Wow, we have no concern that your cancer will ever come back!" kind of healing. But I'll take what we've got: My husband is still here, and I'm not living alone. It's a good answer from a good, good Father. And I still thank God every night for his healing.

Through it all, I've been reminded of how great my Father's love is for me. He is faithful! I don't really like the constant checking of numbers, the "is this the month it comes back" question always in the back of our minds. But when I look back through the journal entries I wrote during John's treatment, I see God's faithfulness and love, time and time again. He never ceases to amaze me.

Reflect and Respond

Has there been a time when you've had to dig deep to grab hold of hope?

_____

_____

_____

What promise can you find in the Bible that will help you hold on?

_____

_____

_____

Nancy Holte loves to laugh and considers it critical for human survival. Believing that laughter is the best medicine inspires Nancy to share Jesus with love and laughter. More of Nancy's writing can be found on her blog at nancyholte.com.

6

Tenacious Hope Is Anchored In God's Faithfulness

ANDREA CHRISTENSON

"But you, Lord, are a compassionate and gracious God, slow to anger, abounding in love and faithfulness."

Psalm 86:5 (NIV)

On a cold, blustery, and snowy Saturday morning, I completely blew it. Ignoring the time and disregarding the appointment I had scheduled with my husband, I instead chatted an extra hour with the women seated in the youth room at our church.

I'd like to think my situation was unique, but, to be honest, human beings are constantly letting each other down. We casually blow off our promises. We say hurtful things. We screw up. We give up on each other when expectations are not met to our satisfaction. We are unfaithful to each other and unfaithful to God.

In my purse beside me on that snowy winter morning, my phone lit up with texts. "Where are you? Have you left yet? Will you be here on time?" Not knowing whether to be angry at my carelessness or worried for my safety, my husband was justified in wondering if I would even get to our appointment at all.

I failed to keep my promise to him, and, in doing so, put a chink in our relationship. On that morning, in that youth room, I proved myself unfaithful.

Thankfully, unfaithfulness is not a part of God's character. Instead, God's faithfulness is a hallmark of his perfection. Time and time again, Scripture gives examples of God's perfect faithfulness, first to the nation of Israel and later to all of us who call on his name. He promised Abraham a son, and a great nation through that son. Though they scoffed at this promise, Abraham and his wife Sarah eventually welcomed a child into their arms. Through this son, Isaac, would come the nation of Israel.

Throughout biblical history we continue to see God's faithfulness. We see God faithfully releasing the Israelites from their bondage in Egypt. Then, we see him providing food and water for the Israelites in the wilderness after their escape. He provided the water, quail, and manna daily even though they complained at every step of that 40-year journey.

Over several hundred years, through the words of the prophets, we see God faithfully promising to send us a Messiah, one who would save his people from their sins and slavery. And, ultimately, we see the fulfillment of his promise when he sends his son, Jesus, to die on the cross for us. A death that freed us from the tyranny of sin. A death that restored perfect communion with God.

Joshua 23:14 (NIV) tells us: "You know with all your heart and soul that not one of all the good promises the Lord your God gave you has failed. Every promise has been fulfilled; not one has failed."

In the gospels, Luke says it even more succinctly: "No word from God will ever fail" (Luke 1:37, NIV).

God always keeps his word to us. Whenever we need him, God is always there for us, and he is always on time. He never gives up on any of us, even when we've given up on him. He forgives our sins; he restores our souls. And, amazingly, he does this even though we don't and never will deserve it.

Romans 5:8 (NIV) says, "But God demonstrates his own love for us in this, while we were yet sinners, Christ died for us."

This is very good news for someone like me. Daily, I fail in my relationship with my husband and with others around me. Daily, I return to God, because his faithful love and forgiveness offers hope, whether I deserve it or not. Unlike me, God is always faithful.

You can have this confidence, too. God's word never fails. Our tenacious hope is anchored in God's faithfulness. We know God keeps his promises, and we know his faithfulness endures even when our own faithfulness flags.

When I finally (and safely) joined my husband at our appointment that winter morning, I saw the love and faithfulness of God take on flesh. Through his own tenacious hope in the Lord, my husband forgave my broken promise and was able to let go of the hurt I caused. I am grateful God continues to refine me, making me more and more into a woman after his own heart.

Until the time I am made perfect, I am glad I can rest in the faithfulness of God.

Reflect and Respond

How has God shown himself faithful to you?

_____

_____

_____

Where have you seen God's promises fulfilled in your life?

_____

_____

_____

Was there ever a time someone demonstrated God's faithfulness to you?

_____

_____

_____

Andrea Christenson is an avid coffee enthusiast, book lover, and–at her core–a writer who seeks to connect to the heart of her readers and point them toward God. She lives with her husband and two daughters in western Wisconsin. You can find Andrea online at AndreaChristenson.com.

7

Tenacious Hope Is Anchored In the Word of God

CINDY DULLUM

"Let us hold fast the confession of our hope without wavering, for He who promised is faithful."

Hebrews 10:23 (ESV)

I remember that time of my life as if it happened yesterday. You may be able to relate. There are times in our lives that leave an imprint upon our souls. Important times. Life-changing times. During that season of life, I watched two close family members as they journeyed together through life with brain tumors. Cancer. Tears. Chemo. Radiation. Hospitals. More cancer. More chemo. More radiation. More tears.

I was only in my twenties, and though it should have been a time of fun, adventure, and new beginnings, these two death sentences consumed my thoughts. My heart ached. Already a young mother of three, my fourth child was born during those dark days. Even as we ushered in a new beginning in our own lives, I watched my loved ones as they spent their final days on earth. Six months after his Uncle Dave passed away, my nephew, Ryan, joined him at heavens' gates.

Now, so many years later, I see the evidence of that difficult time in the verses scribbled on the margins of my tattered Bible. And in them, I see God's tenacious hope revealed. You see, even when life seemed hopeless, and I felt consumed by the darkness of those days, God's Word brought me truth. As John 14:18 (RSV) says, "I will not leave you desolate; I will come to you."

Tenacious hope grabs onto Scripture as if reaching for a lifeline in a raging sea. White-knuckled, unwavering. Trusting each inspired word of God—his love letter to us.

Psalms 121:1-2 (RSV) says, "I lift up my eyes to the hills. From whence does my help come from? My help comes from the Lord, who made heaven and earth."

That Scripture became my buoy, and I sang the words until they became my truth. God, the one who would help me! Help us.

Hebrews 10:23 instructs us "to hold fast the confession of our hope without wavering, for He who promised is faithful." With fierce conviction, boldness, faith, and hope, we diligently grab on to God's promises, for he is with us in these moments. He is the one whom the Psalmist proclaims in Psalms 18:1-2: Our strength, rock, fortress, deliverer, refuge, shield, the hope of our salvation, and our stronghold!

Through his Word, God gave me everything that I needed during those difficult days. Since then, I have referred to those scribbled verses countless times as the enemy has tried to steal my peace. Each time, God's truth has been cemented even deeper into my soul.

Reflect and Respond

What battle are you facing today?

_____

_____

_____

Are there areas of your life that feel overwhelming today? God is here. He is with you. Search Scripture to find the verse that will speak hope into your heart.

_____

_____

_____

Dear Jesus, Help us to see you in the situations we encounter. Make your promises known to us, that we would have tenacious hope. As we trust you with our heart's desires, may you speak truth into us. We believe you. We want to have an unwavering, steady hope. Thank you for your Word, your promises, and your truth. We love you! Amen.

Cindy Dullum has a passion to see women grow in their faith as they walk with Jesus. She enjoys spending time with family, working as a high school data management secretary, writing, speaking, spending time in God's Word, concerts, retreats, and conferences.

8

Tenacious Hope Is Anchored In
God's Promise to Never Leave Me

LIZZIE LINDBERG

"And I will ask the Father, and he will give you another helper,
to be with you forever,
even the Spirit of truth, whom the world cannot receive,
because it neither sees him nor knows him.
You know him, for he dwells in you and will be with you."

John 14:16-17 (ESV)

This isn't what it's supposed to look like, I thought as I exited my kids' bedroom for the thousandth time. They were supposed to go to sleep, and I was supposed to have a partner to help with bedtime. *It's not fair; it's someone else's turn,* rang over and over in my head. Finally, fully dismayed, I crumpled into a pile on my own bedroom floor. It had been years since the death of my husband and co-parent, yet tonight the single-mom life had dropped me deep in the dirt of loneliness, frustration, and exhaustion. Being mom to my kids is one of the greatest privileges I have on this earth, and most of the time I am incredibly thankful. But at bedtime? Bedtime is the worst.

"No, you can't have another drink, or read another book, or play with the toy. It's time for sleep. Why are you up? Go back to bed. Just go to bed. Go. Bed. Now." I would count how many times I say these things in a single night, but I would end up putting myself to sleep.

Eventually, though, they always do fall asleep. I win that battle almost every night. But then comes the true battle: the one in my head. In the dark, at the end of the day, the hum of busyness grows quiet and the reality of my aloneness feels deafening.

This isn't what it's supposed to look like . . . it isn't fair.

Years ago, after the kids fell asleep, my husband and I would have time to ourselves to watch or read something, talk, or just do nothing next to one another. But now it's just me—alone, tired, sad, and a little angry at the injustice of it all.

It's in moments like that, however, that I've found the Holy Spirit speaks the loudest. A little nudge at first, and then almost as if he were whispering in my ear, I hear him say, "Child, I'm with you."

God has promised to never, ever leave us. It's written all over his word (Deuteronomy 31:6, 1 Chronicles 28:20, Psalm 55:22, Isaiah 41:10, Matthew 28:20, and Hebrews 13:5, to name a few). He didn't promise that we wouldn't face hardship or that the world would be fair. In fact, he told us the opposite would be true! No, he didn't promise ease in this life; he promised to be with us through whatever happened:

"And I will ask the Father, and he will give you another Helper, to *be with you forever*, even the Spirit of truth, whom the world cannot receive, because it neither sees him nor knows him. You know him, for *he dwells with you and will be in you*. I will not leave you as orphans; I will come to you. Yet a little while and the world will see me no more, but you will see me. Because I live, you also will live. In that day you will know that I am in my Father, and you in me, and I in you" (John 14:16-20, ESV, emphasis mine).

God is not my husband. He's not a literal, tangible person who's going to put my kids to bed if I can't figure it out. I'm not trying to say that he is a replacement for an earthly co-parent. What I do hold on to, however, is that he's always going to be the one to whom I can talk no matter what. He might not be the MVP in the children's bedtime game, but he will be my rock, provide my comfort, and protect my rest in the darkness after the lights go out. His promise is the reason that I have hope for right now and for the days to come.

When my focus is set on the negatives of whatever is happening in my life, the darkness can keep me feeling lonely and blue. But when I fix my eyes on God, remembering his promises, I can take hold of hope—the kind of hope that lifts me from where I lay and pulls me into motion like a father's hand reaching down to his child. This is the kind of hope that brings peace as I rest, knowing that I have nothing to fear because he protects me even while I sleep (Psalm 4:8).

Reflect and Respond

At what time of the day do you most often find yourself feeling lonely?

_____

_____

_____

Does it help you to know that God has promised that he will never leave you alone? Why or why not?

_____

_____

_____

Take a second to reflect on the verses that confirm God's promise. Is there one that sticks out to you that can help you when you need an extra dose of tenacious hope?

_____

_____

_____

Lizzie Lindberg is a mom to two little boys and a young widow. As a part-time Communications Director, she cultivates creativity and consistency. When she's home, Lizzie excels at making mayonnaise, composing dinosaur noises, and singing her ABCs. Lizzie writes about motherhood, grief, and God's faithfulness at lizziejlindberg.com.

9

Tenacious Hope Is Anchored In Eternity

ANNA HENKE

"He will wipe every tear from their eyes.
There will be no more death or mourning
or crying or pain, for the old order of things has passed away."
Revelation 21:4 (NIV)

I've always been a dreamer who believed in fairy tales. Stories speak to my heart. As a child, my favorite thing to do was to turn the pages of a book. To this day, I get lost in worlds of words.

The song from the Disney version of *Cinderella*, "A Dream Is a Wish Your Heart Makes," came to mind the other day when I was cleaning. It got me thinking about dreams and wishes—the wishes I've made in the past, the dreams I have now, and the hope I have for the future.

As a child of ten, my most cherished wish was simple: to be free from chronic pain. I prayed about it. I daydreamed about a future without it. I even went so far as to wish upon a star.

It's a wish that took me a long time to let go of. I used to believe, for some inexplicable reason, that when I was older I would miraculously get better— that all my problems would be solved. But as the saying goes, if wishes were horses, beggars would ride. I have struggled with chronic pain for my entire life. And it's been hard. I won't deny it.

In high school, I lost the use of my legs. In college, I had seizures. In my adult life, I get migraines and still experience ever-present joint pain. The pain is a constant reminder of just how imperfect this world is.

However, I don't wish away the pain anymore. I know that it's part of my story. Every heroine has a trial, and this is mine. It's made me stronger. It's made me appreciate true joy. More importantly, that constant reminder of our broken world has led me back to God every step of the way. It's led me to place my hope, not in the things of this world, but in the promise of eternity.

You see, the thing about wishes and dreams is that they are limited by our imagination. In real life, there's no such thing as a fairy godmother, and thank goodness for that. We have something so much better.

Think about it: Sure, Cinderella got to go to the ball, but she lost everything when the clock struck twelve. It was all a wisp of magic. None of it was real. The carriage was really a pumpkin, and that's what it remained.

Now, my hope is not merely a wish. It's not even a dream—because I chose it, consciously. I replaced fairy godmothers with the almighty God a long time ago. The hope I cling to now is real. It's tenacious. It says in God's Word that there will be no more tears and no more pain (Revelation 21:4). And I believe it!

My hope now is anchored in eternity—it has no limit. There is no uncertainty, because it's not magic; his promises are true. God has demonstrated that to me time and time again. He restored my legs. He healed my seizures. He grants me joy in the midst of struggle.

My hope in God, in the promise of an eternity without tears, without pain, and without death, is what gives me strength to live out my story through the rough middle chapters. Pain is part of my narrative, but I know and trust in my happy ending. It's better than anything I could have imagined, and I can't wait to live it out.

Reflect and Respond

What part of your story do you need to embrace in order to move forward in hope?

_____

_____

_____

Do you think about eternity? If so, does it comfort you amid life's challenges? Why or why not?

_____

_____

_____

Anna Henke loves telling stories—her own and those of others. After six years in the publishing field, she founded the copywriting business The Resident Writer, LLC, where she works with female entrepreneurs to refine their messaging and help them reach their goals. She spends most of her downtime reading or being with those she loves. Anna lives in Eden Prairie, MN. To learn more about her and her story, visit theresidentwriter.com.

10

Tenacious Hope Is Anchored In
His Deliverance

LENAE BULTHUIS

"May the God of hope fill you with all joy and peace as you trust in him,
so that you may overflow with hope by the power of the Holy Spirit."

Romans 15:13 (NIV)

Adoption was never the plan. When our family chose to be foster parents, we simply wanted to give a temporary home to kids who needed one. And though my husband and our three daughters who were in middle and high school treasured each child, it was different with Jeremiah.* For us, Jeremiah was a forever-family kind of different.

Jeremiah's biological dad thought so, too. So when he asked if we would adopt his son, we replied with an immediate and unanimous yes. Though adoption was not our original plan, we were all in.

Have you ever had a time when your hopes were raised, only to be stripped away?

That's our story. Hearts and home prepared for adoption, the system chose a different path for Jeremiah. We were stunned and crushed. Our hearts were ripped by the separation.

In light of our pain, I can only imagine the grief of the Shunammite woman written about in the Old Testament (2 Kings 4:8-37). Her hopes were raised when the prophet Elisha told her that next year she would hold a son in her arms. It was more than she thought possible or dared to dream. She had no son;

her husband was old. But against all logic, a son was born! The child grew but then suddenly died.

Her hopes had been raised, only to be stripped away! Grieved and distressed, she went to Elisha and said, "Didn't I tell you, 'Don't raise my hopes'?" (2 Kings 4:28).

Hopes raised. Hopes ripped away. It's not unique to Mrs. Shunammite. It's our story too. Can you identify?

Your pregnancy test reads positive, and then a miscarriage happens.

You land your dream job, only to lose it to a merger or a move.

Your scans read clear—until they don't.

You make the final car payment one month, only to have the cylinder head gasket blow up the next.

Your relationship with one friend is mended, only to be blindsided and betrayed by another friend.

Elisha went to the lifeless boy, prayed to God, and lay prostrate "on the boy, mouth to mouth, eyes to eyes, hands to hands," (2 Kings 4:34). Miraculously, the child was restored to life.

Lives change when we stop anchoring our hope to circumstances (which is really no hope at all) and choose to lay prostrate and surrendered to the God of hope. The dead are brought to life when hope is found in a relationship with Jesus Christ.

The next time your hopes are raised and then ripped away, raise them up again by giving them to God, the source of true hope. Remember this HOPE acronym.

H. Have a heart-to-heart with God. Be honest about how you feel and what this situation looks like from your perspective. He invites you to do just that! "Cast all your anxiety on him because he cares for you," (1 Peter 5:7).

O. Open God's Word. Not sure where to begin? Start in the book of John or study the Bible with friends. Ask a woman of faith to read it with you and pray for you. "You are my refuge and my shield; I have put my hope in your word," (Psalm 119:114).

P. Place your hope in God. Turn your eyes from your troubles to the truth of who he is, all he is doing, and what he has promised you. "'For I know the plans I have for you,' declares the Lord, 'plans to prosper you and not to harm you, plans to give you hope and a future,'" (Jeremiah 29:11).

E. Expect God to deliver. Psalm 33:17 says, "A horse is a vain hope for deliverance." So are social media, shopping sprees, sweets, and spirits. Instead, find your hope in him: "Wait in hope for the Lord; he is our help and our shield," (Psalm 33:20).

Reflect and Respond

Where or in what do you regularly place your hope for comfort, control, and security?

_____

_____

_____

What would it look like to redirect that hope toward God?

_____

_____

_____

Lenae Bulthuis is on staff with GEMS Girls' Clubs, and counts it grace to blog and speak about faith, family, and farming. She lives with her husband Mike on a grain and livestock farm in west central Minnesota where she reads, writes, and wraps her arms around their grandlittles.

*Name has been changed. All Scripture references are taken from the New International Version.

11

Tenacious Hope Is Anchored In
My Father's Love

ANNA FRIENDT

"May your unfailing love be with us, Lord,
even as we put our hope in you."

Psalm 33:20-22 (NIV)

One summer, as a young girl, I attended Bible camp. In chapel, the worship leader transitioned from one song to the next by asking us children to envision our fathers standing in front of us and to hold up our hands like we were asking to be picked up. I lifted my hands for a brief moment and immediately pulled them back as I remembered that I didn't have any memories of this kind of daddy-daughter relationship. None. And that hurt.

I knew that my biological father hadn't treated me the way a father should; he was jailed when I was 3 because he had sexually abused me. There was no way I'd reach my hands out to him. Between the ages of 3 and 6, I was in foster care and then the family that adopted me...well, I didn't know how to reach out to my new dad, either.

I ran out of that chapel so fast. The next thing I knew, I was back in my cabin bunk bed with my arms held tightly to my body, fists clenched as tears fell. I did not believe the promise that the Father loved me. Instead, I felt hopeless.

Eventually my adoptive dad became "daddy" to me. He reflected the Father's love well. It didn't matter where I came from or what had happened to me. My daddy loved me and I believed it. I knew if I needed a hug or encouragement, all I had to do was reach out and ask. I could come empty-handed. However, I still struggled to know that God felt the same way toward me.

I gained a deeper understanding of God's fatherly love for me in February of 2016. One day as I was helping my parents out at the house, I got a glimpse of my daddy sitting in his chair from my spot at the table in the dining room. The sunlight that poured into the room was shining on him as he raised his hands in worship. Both hands, empty and facing upward. He had nothing to offer but his heart.

Four days before, we had found out he had stomach cancer and were hopeful for a treatment plan.

Three days before, he told me he was very, very sick.

And just one day before, he told me he was dying.

The day I saw him lift his empty hands was the day he read the full report—it was terminal. The cancer had already spread throughout his entire abdomen, covering all of his major organs.

When I saw him worship, I realized this: His hope was not in the healing; his hope was in the Healer. The circumstances didn't matter, nor the outcome. It was simple. Jesus was the hope that motivated his hands to be raised in worship as he exchanged his burden for the promises of God, given to him through our deliverer, the one we put our hope in.

As Psalm 40:17 (NIV) says, "As for me, I am poor and needy, but the Lord takes thought for me. You are my help and my deliverer; do not delay, O my God!"

Daddy's hands were empty. What did he have to offer? He was in great need and had nothing. All he had was his desire for Jesus. Because he knew that the Father's love for him was real, he knew that if he simply reached out, hope would carry him through and deliver him from whatever he faced. Even death.

Psalm 40:17 is my heart's cry when my childhood hurts rise up and overwhelm me. It is my cry when the grief of losing my daddy becomes too crippling. Sometimes that is all I have to offer in worship: a cry of total surrender from the heart. I have learned that to reach out is to choose to believe and trust that the Father does in fact love me, even when I come to him empty-handed or with burdens. We do not have to be strong to open our hands and ask for help. Our strength comes when we open our hands for help and the help arrives. Jesus is our helper, our strength, and our hope.

Reflect and Respond

Do you believe God loves you and that you can come to him empty-handed? If not, start there. Open your hands and ask him to help you receive his love for you.

_____

_____

_____

What hurts do you need the Father to deliver you from? Pray through Psalm 40:17. Reach out and ask him to pick you up.

_____

_____

_____

Anna Friendt is an artist, writer, and speaker. God used the creative arts to facilitate healing from her past and has enabled her to share that same hope with others. She is the founder of a nonprofit, Anchor 13 Studio, and her personal creative works can be found at annafriendt.com.

TENACIOUS HOPE

Is Greater Than...

12

TENACIOUS HOPE IS GREATER THAN the Enemy's Lies

ANGIE KUTZER

"I say to myself, 'The LORD is my inheritance;
therefore, I will hope in him!'"

Lamentations 3:24 (NLT)

Have you ever been scared about the future? Do you worry that you may not have what it takes to conquer the next thing you feel God calling you to?

From time to time, I think we all feel uncertain. I imagine that most people have experienced a season of concern about their own abilities to carry through with something new and challenging.

The enemy certainly schemes for us to have a less than ample amount of confidence in ourselves, which can make us doubt God's plan for our lives. We may not be doubting God, but rather doubting ourselves and our capability to do certain things.

For me, an unexpected and unplanned opportunity to go back to school recently presented itself. This particular life plunge has been brewing for 12 years.

A long time ago, when I was a staff member at a church, I often thought about my unquenchable thirst for more of the Lord. I wondered if I would make a good pastor. Then, the enemy told me, "You are not smart enough to go to seminary. You are too scatterbrained to succeed. With toddlers at home, you cannot go back to school."

A few years later, as a family struggle brought me back into a place of deep longing for more of Jesus, I thought again about advancing my Christian knowledge. The enemy told me, "You are not good enough to be a church leader. You are not qualified for a position in the church because of your past."

And again, a few years down the road, when a career change was needed and it was time for me to figure out a new path, I thought about my love for Jesus and how I live to share that love with everyone I encounter. But the enemy stopped me again. In my mind I heard him saying, "You cannot help others when you cannot conquer your own anxiety. You are not capable of guiding others through life challenges when sometimes your own life is a real mess. Girl, how could you possibly think that you—broken, exhausted you—could handle leading and counseling others?"

Each time I thought about going to seminary, negative thoughts and possible undesirable outcomes constantly flowed through my mind.

Well, here I am today, once again contemplating going to seminary, while raising two middle-schoolers and working full time. And here are just a few of the lies that I hear in my head today:

You cannot handle all of this!

I respond with, "I can do all this through him who gives me strength," Philippians 4:13 (NIV).

Are you doing this to prove something or to show off on Earth?

My response is "The world and its desires pass away, but whoever does the will of God lives forever," 1 John 2:17 (NIV).

You are not capable of maintaining your family relationships and keeping them healthy while taking on so much. Your home will not be able to function if you follow this huge calling.

And my faith responds, "We now have this light shining in our hearts, but we ourselves are like fragile clay jars containing this great treasure. This makes it clear that our great power is from God, not from ourselves," 2 Corinthians 4:7 (NLT).

This time I am strong enough to know that these lies are untrue!

This is the calling of God on my life, and he will renew me over and over again. God will give me and my family the strength to make it through this potentially trying time in a way that will make us even stronger!

God has set each of us up to prosper and teach and share and love—all things the enemy wants to derail.

If you are in the midst of fighting for what the Lord is calling you toward, trust me, the negative and discouraging messages in your mind are certainly the lies of the enemy.

We must remain full of tenacious hope! We are the vessel entrusted to carry and pour out the promises of God to others every day.

Stand firm in the many truths that you know about God's strength, determination, and blessings. Jesus is the way, the truth, and the life! He will lead us to all the promises God has for us. He will sustain us through the trials.

As I write this, I am starting seminary study in four weeks. I am overwhelmingly excited, deeply proud, and, yes, quite anxious. But I know in the depths of my heart and soul that I can trust God to see me through this time and to make me into who he intends me to be

So, dear child of God, be persistent in your efforts to claim the hope earned for you by Jesus Christ. Cling to the truth that God heals us, surrounds us with love and mercy, and renews us, and be determined to act on God's will for you!

Stand firm on the truth that hope is greater than the enemy's lies.

Reflect and Respond

In what areas of your life is the enemy whispering lies to you?

_____

_____

_____

What scriptures can you use to combat those lies? Take a few moments and ask God to open your eyes to what he would have you believe about yourself.

_____

_____

_____

Angie Kutzer lives in Bismarck, ND, with her husband and two sons. Angie spends her free time singing at church and volunteering at the state penitentiary. Angie is a blogger and freelance writer and started her ministry, "Frommylifetoyourheart," out of her passion to share her life and faith. Angie strives to inspire others to live a life of joy and find happiness in all circumstances. She started her studies at Luther Seminary in fall of 2018.

13

Tenacious Hope Is Greater Than Grief

BECKY MEYERSON

"Now may God, the inspiration and fountain of hope, fill you to overflowing with uncontainable joy and perfect peace as you trust in him. And may the power of the Holy Spirit continually surround your life with his super abundance until you radiate with hope!"

Romans 15:13 (TPT)

It was the middle of a rough season, and my heart was heavy with grief. My parents had passed away within four months of each other, and I was trying to be gentle with myself through the process of grief. So when my morning devotional brought me to Romans 15:13, I had an honest conversation with God.

"God, I do have confident hope that my parents have eternal life in you. But I am not overflowing with joy or peace. I am not sure that is even possible right now."

Reading God's Word and listening to the voice of the Holy Spirit can be difficult as you travel through the various stages of grief. It's okay. Give yourself grace. Choose a "tried and true" devotional and keep faithfully reading, even when it doesn't seem like anything is really penetrating. That is what I had to do. Learning something new from the Word just seemed too difficult, so I grabbed a well-used yearly devotional and kept my sunrise reading routine.

As I sat quietly that morning, I sensed a shift in me as I settled into the verse and revisited each word. I realized three truths that morning:

1. I don't need to drum up hope in my heart. God himself is both the inspiration and the fountain of hope. I can anchor my grieving heart in him.
2. I don't have to produce my own joy and peace. God promises to fill me up as I trust in him.
3. The Holy Spirit surrounds me with his power. I will radiate with hope as I allow that encircling power to fill me.

From that morning on, I turned Romans 15:13 into my daily prayer.

"God, thank you for the confidence of eternal life. I know Mom and Dad are in heaven with you. Lord, I ask you to fill me to overflowing with uncontainable joy and perfect peace. I will continually keep my trust in you and my eyes looking upward. Holy Spirit, I invite you to surround me with your power. I will continue to give myself time and grace to grieve, knowing that you are my God of hope."

As I prayed that prayer over the next few weeks, I could sense my heart lighten, my spirit soar, and my life radiate with hope. The same can happen to you.

Let your heart rest in the God of hope. He is always true to his character and does not waver from his values and commitments to you. You don't need to struggle to grab hope, be joyful, or obtain peace. Just receive them as gifts from God. Let him be your inspiration and your fountain of hope.

Reflect and Respond

If you have recently lost a loved one, have you given yourself permission to grieve in your own way and in your own timeline?

_____

_____

_____

Oftentimes, we experience other kinds of grief in our lives. How do you handle losses such as a job or a trusted friend?

_____

_____

_____

During seasons of grief, how will you grasp for hope, joy, and peace in your life?

_____

_____

_____

Becky Meyerson is passionate about writing and teaching from the Word of God. She is wife to Scott, mom to four daughters and two sons-in-law, and Nana to five beautiful grandchildren. She loves to garden, try new recipes, and gather family and friends around her table. You can find her latest adventures in faith, food, and family on her website, evergreen.study.

14

Tenacious Hope Is Greater Than the Things I Can't Control

TABBY FINTON

"God has not given us a spirit of fear, but of power, love, and a sound mind."
2 Timothy 1:7 (NIV)

I've ridden a confidence roller coaster for much of my life. As a child, I was happy and innocently self-assured, and although I experienced many bumps during adolescence, I ended my high school years on a high. I was young, but I was bold as a lion! I received a call to the ministry when I was 16 years old, and I watched God do incredible things right before my eyes. My faith was large. Even though I knew there would be challenges, I felt sure that I could take them on through God's strength.

I ventured off to the great state of Minnesota for Bible college at 17. I didn't know one person within a 300-mile radius, but I loved everything about college when I arrived! I was very outgoing, and felt enamored with the big city and the amazing people that surrounded me. I chose a full load of credits and led worship in churches with a small traveling team. The full-load was much more difficult than I had anticipated, but I pushed through the challenge. No one on my ministry team wanted to take on the leadership responsibilities of organizing and scheduling, so I said I would do it. Why not, right? But one of the two men in our group didn't think that women should take on leadership roles, and he consistently shared his opinion. I offered again and again to allow him to lead, but he didn't want the job. He just didn't want me doing it.

For some reason, I allowed that to knock me off of my proverbial pedestal, and my confidence floundered for years.

Around that same time, my future husband Steve and I were serving as volunteers with teens in a youth group, working under an amazing youth pastor named Leo, who profoundly affected us. We had only been married five days when Leo died of cancer that had been discovered three months prior to his death. He was 24 years old.

I became consumed by fear. In my mind, it wasn't a matter of *if* Steve was going to die, but *when*. We didn't have cell phones back then, and if Steve was more than a few minutes late coming home from classes or work, I could be found calling hospital emergency rooms to see if he'd been admitted as a patient. Unmitigated fear began to wrap its coils around me; I felt I could hardly breathe at times.

Working alongside an incredibly critical coworker made things even more difficult. According to her, I couldn't do anything right, and I backed away from many leadership opportunities because I felt intimidated and feared rejection. Steve and I were only in our twenties, but Leo's death at such a young age caused me to become consumed by fear. Struggling to combat such overwhelming feelings, my fear began to emerge as anger, most often unleashed on my husband.

After my second child was born, I often awoke abruptly from sleep to make sure the boys were still alive. I envisioned images of both of them in little white suits lying together in a small, wooden casket. Each successive experience I faced knocked my confidence down and caused my fears to heighten. I felt suffocated.

It wasn't until a friend explained that I was carrying a spirit of fear, and helped me see how I could be free, that I finally felt renewed hope. I cried out to God, renounced fear, and felt him release me from fear's terrible grip.

That life-changing conversation with my friend happened many years ago, and although the enemy still tries to trick me into giving into fear at times, I recognize his schemes. If the enemy can keep us cowering in the corner, we'll never step out and accomplish the bold and courageous acts of faith God has created us to undertake. During those years in which I was captive to fear, my effectiveness in God's kingdom was limited. Although I still did things for God, I didn't realize until afterward that fear was keeping me from accomplishing all that God had planned for me. I will not invite or assume chains of fear back into my life. As John 8:36 says, "Whom the son sets free is free indeed!" (NIV, paraphrased). With God's help, we can *choose* to be free from the things that bind us.

Reflect and Respond

How have fear, anger, and intimidation tried to cling to you, as they did to me?

_____

_____

_____

How can you respond to God today to be released from bonds that attempt to hold you captive?

_____

_____

_____

Tabby Finton is a lifelong lover of God, and she is passionate about his purposes. She's a credentialed minister and loves to speak, write, and encourage. She is mom to three sons and married to Steve, Lead Pastor at Abundant Life Church in Blaine, Minnesota.

15

Tenacious Hope Is Greater Than My Insecurities

KRISTIN DEMERY

"For when I am weak, then I am strong."
2 Corinthians 12:10 (NLT)

Thump. From above, the loud crash reverberating from the second floor could be heard over the low hum of conversation in the main-floor living room. Smiling nonchalantly, my husband and I continued to converse pleasantly with new friends from the church we had been attending for a few months.

After a momentary pause, the mysterious thump was heard again. Pause. *Thump.* Pause. *Thump.*

Finally, one of the men looked at us. "Uh—what's going on? What's making that noise?"

"Oh, that?" we shrugged. "That's Elise."

Honestly, the fact that our toddler was leaping from a dresser to the floor was, at this point, no big deal. This was the child who scrambled out of her crib before she could talk, the one who swung from the curtains until they crashed to the floor, the one who climbed the bookcase until it ripped out of the drywall. This was the child that required the use of a lock on her closet after she scrambled up to the highest shelf, and who viewed escaping out of her bedroom as an Olympic event. This was the same child who, perhaps most memorably, urinated down the vent during her potty training phase. After scrubbing out the vent, we calmly scissored off the feet on her one-piece pajamas, zipped her up the back, and sent her back to bed.

Life with Elise was an adventure, and a few extra jumps at bedtime were par for the course.

But my laissez faire attitude that evening wasn't the response I had always had throughout my parenting journey. When I was pregnant, I remember having somewhat amorphous dreams about what my child might be like. I hoped he or she would like books—like me—that they would love Jesus and love others. I don't think I had anything else on my proverbial "list," which is probably why God had a big belly laugh at my expense when he sent an active, outgoing, expressive little person my way. At no time did I envision a child who would have me Googling things that only other people's cats seem to do.

But when you have a child, you quickly realize that this child is both fully yours—bone of my bone, flesh of my flesh—and yet uniquely their own person. While you can modify behavior or steer them toward a good path, ultimately that child's personality and perspective on life is their own. That's both terrifying and exhilarating. And so I found myself, as a young mother, completely overwhelmed at the prospect of parenting a child who seemed so different from me. I loved her, but I felt embarrassed and overwhelmed when she acted certain ways, did certain things. I'd like to think that I'm a strong person, but I felt keenly my weakness in the face of her own strong will.

The funny thing about weaknesses is that it is in those moments that we experience most profoundly the power of God. Consider what Paul says in 2 Corinthians 12:8-10 (NLT):

> "Three different times I begged the Lord to take it away. Each time he said, 'My grace is all you need. My power works best in weakness.' So now I am glad to boast about my weaknesses, so that the power of Christ can work through me. That's why I take pleasure in my weaknesses, and in the insults, hardships, persecutions, and troubles that I suffer for Christ. For when I am weak, then I am strong."

For too many years, I misread that. I always assumed that when I am weak, he is strong. And that's true, that the power of Christ works best in weakness—but it's awe-inspiring that the very thing that makes us weak, also makes us strong.

Read it again: *For when I am weak, then I am strong.*

And so we find our hope, not in trying to be strong or figure it all ourselves. Not in pretending that our little gift from God really does wear a halo or that we never find ourselves sobbing inconsolably or locked in a bathroom with our own anger. Not in ignoring our fears and frustrations, wondering if we're the only one who can't figure out how to parent a precocious child. No, our strength comes in admitting that we don't have all the answers—but we know the one who does. That when we can lay down our pride and admit to our friends, or even just to ourselves, that we are imperfect and struggling—oh, the freedom that brings. Tenacious hope is greater than my insecurities, because I can stand firm in the security that is found in the faithfulness of God. When we are weak, we are strong.

The great thing about God is that he loves to surprise us. You know what I love best about Elise? She's smart and funny and creative, but my favorite characteristic is that she really does love well, just as I imagined she would. (She likes books, too, but that's just a bonus at this point.) God really did give me the items on my list—and then he improved the list.

Reflect and Respond

Sometimes our own insecurities can cause our hope to falter. What would happen if you saw your weaknesses and insecurities as moments for God's strength to prevail? How would that change your response?

_____

_____

_____

Have you ever seen God respond to your hopes and prayers in unexpected ways? How did that alter your perspective?

_____

_____

_____

Kristin Demery is married to her best friend, Tim, and is a mom to three girls. A grammar geek and Jane Austen addict, Kristin has a background in journalism that has led to many roles, from managing a social networking site for moms to working as an editorial assistant for an academic journal. Her greatest dream, however, is to live a life of extravagant generosity. Kristin's work has been featured in diverse publications, including the _St. Cloud Times_, _ROI Business_ magazine, _USA Today_, and _(in)courage_. She's also an advisor, editor, and writer for Bridging the Gap. Kristin loves staying up way too late, spending sun-soaked days at Madeline Island with her family, sipping campfire mochas, thrifting, and gift giving. You can find Kristin writing about mistakes, motherhood, and the power of grace on her blog at theruthexperience.com.

16

Tenacious Hope Is Greater Than

My Fears

SANDY MCKEOWN

"So do not fear, for I am with you; do not be dismayed, for I am your God.
I will strengthen you and help you;
I will uphold you with my righteous right hand."

Isaiah 41:10 (NIV)

It can be a herculean effort to get five active kids into the car, buckled up and ready to ride peacefully for just a short, one-hour trip. How, in the name of our mighty Lord, did Noah wrangle two of every kind of creature onto the ark, into their perspective places, and ready to ride out the storm of the ages?

Genesis 9:2 gives us a hint: "The fear and dread of you will fall upon all the beasts of the earth . . ." The animals didn't fear him! Not until after the flood did God give them this fear. Noah and his sons could probably walk right alongside them without any difficulty as he guided them to their imminent ark ride. It was very convenient for the task at hand.

An absence of fear worked nicely for Noah's walk of obedience. But fear is something every person experiences in life. And fear can stop us from doing what we need to do. It's an emotion that cannot be shrugged off, but it can be tenaciously tucked away as we determine to do what needs to be done.

Headed home one hot summer day, I decided to take the back roads due to excessive traffic on the main highways. I was enjoying the much quieter roads, so pleased with myself for remembering to avoid all the commotion on the interstate, when I drove around a curve in the road and saw a lone doe standing right in the middle of the road. Not moving. Still as could be. I had plenty of time to slow down and stop—it was a fluke she had positioned herself to allow for a strategic stop of my car. Or was it?

I slowed to a gentle stop about seven feet from her, and we locked eyes. Her big, beautiful doe eyes did not move even a little. "Okay, what's the plan here?" I voiced aloud, even though I knew she couldn't hear or understand me. Then I saw movement in the ditch to my left. A gangly newborn that had not yet learned to walk very gracefully climbed out of the ditch with great effort, noisily scrambled across the road, lanky legs working hard, experiencing a few stumbles along the way, and then disappeared into the reeds and shrubbery on the other side of the road. Once the newborn was safe, the doe broke eye contact with me and quickly followed her young. They were both out of sight in seconds.

The beautiful momma had flagged traffic for her baby.

It was a powerful example to me of momma fierceness, forgetting what fear you have in the moment because it's time to fight for your baby—at any cost.

Why do we fight for our children?

Perhaps a disability is diagnosed with a low quality of life outcome tagged on for your child. We fight for a better future.

A school denies enrollment—and education—due to severity of said disability. We fight for a better future.

A nice guy who is a long way from being ready for marriage wants to marry your daughter. We fight for a better future.

My husband and I fought all three of those battles. They weren't easy, and we battled fear before we faced the tangible fight head on.

Yep. I knew exactly what that momma deer was doing. I understood her courage, her tenacity, and her instinct to do whatever it takes to make sure her baby survives this thing called life. She was fighting for the future of her baby.

The beasts of the earth fear man. This doe feared me and, I'm sure, the large vehicle I was driving, but she stood her ground. She fought for her baby's future.

She had somehow learned—tragically—that cars kill. And she was doing something fearsome to protect her baby.

Facing something that can hurt you with heart racing, with lungs-aren't-getting-enough-air kind of fear. Wishing you didn't have to do it, but there is no other choice . . . if you want something different for your baby.

I'm not altogether sure God bestowed much fear on the lion after the flood. Being on top of the food chain sure helps. There is a confidence about the lion that denotes a powerful position in life, but there is also a bold ferociousness when needed. In the wonderful family movie *Iron Will*, one man who is older and in a comfortable season in life is in awe of a younger man who selflessly put himself at risk and saved another man's life, and he proclaims: "He's got the heart of a lion."

Where do we find that kind of courage for our loved ones?

Again, God's word gives the answer. Psalm 46:1-2 says, "God is our refuge and strength, an ever present help in trouble. Therefore we will not fear."

He shelters and protects. He is powerful and mighty. And he is ours if we ask. We don't have to be alone on that road.

Today I pray for the heart of a lion—and a momma deer. For my kids.

Reflect and Respond

What do you fear?

_____

_____

_____

How might your actions change as you view your own fearful situations through the lens of God's protection and power?

_____

_____

_____

Have you asked the Lord to calm your fears so you can do what needs to be done?

_____

_____

_____

Sandy McKeown and her husband are the parents of five children, three with extra challenges. Sandy uses life experience combined with powerful insight and creative humor to convey true hope to all audiences. You can contact her at sandymckeown. com.

17

Tenacious Hope Is Greater Than My Automatic Negative Thoughts

JAYNE POLI

"For I know the thoughts that I think toward you,
says the LORD, thoughts of peace
and not of evil, to give you a future and a hope."
Jeremiah 29:11 (NKJV)

Several years ago, I was challenged by God to speak only positive things for a month. Even though I believed I spoke positive things most of the time, I was hesitant to take on this challenge. After just the first hour of the monthly commitment, I quickly realized how habitually I spoke negative things about others and myself. As I considered the negative messages that lived on the tip of my tongue, the Lord showed me that my thoughts were the problem. God showed me that I would not be speaking these negative things if I was thinking positive, life-giving thoughts. The overwhelmingly repetitive negative thoughts were so ingrained in my mind. I knew I needed help from the Lord to change the way I thought. I needed to cling to the hope of God through the appropriation of his promises to me.

The hope of God is more than wishful thinking. Hope is akin to faith. Hope is believing in God's love for you. Hope is refusing to see circumstances as "truth" above God's promises. The ability to seek hope and cling to it takes tenacity. The tenacity to train your mind to discount what your eyes see, and instead ask God to give you spiritual eyes, is necessary to grab hold of hope and live in faith.

Hope is not what first comes to my mind when I am faced with a tough situation. If you are like me, typically what pops into your mind are the old thought patterns that you adopted in childhood. As a child, when a disappointment or trial came your way, your little brain came up with a "logical" explanation for why this terrible thing happened to you. Some typical beliefs a child may adopt include:

If I was a good girl, this would not have happened to me.

My parent loves my siblings more than me.

A bad thing will happen after a good thing happens, to even it out.

Logic may tell us that history is a good indicator of the future. However, in the Kingdom of God, and with the authority Jesus gives his children, you can rest assured that the past has no power over your future in him.

Often negative thoughts can seem like second nature, but they are not of God. They are rooted in shame, blame, or striving. Holding onto past failures and disappointments is futile and defeating when God has already put them under the blood of Jesus and chosen to forget them.

Psalms 103:12 says, "As far as the east is from the west, so far has he removed our transgressions from us." This verse shows us that even God chooses to train his thoughts in a positive, life-giving direction. The all-knowing God chooses to forget our sins. It is fascinating to study verses that talk about God's thoughts.

Isaiah 55:8 explains, "'For My thoughts are not your thoughts, nor are your ways My ways,' declares the Lord."

There are many verses about God's thoughts that can and will give you hope, if you choose to accept his words about you, his beloved child. "Many, O LORD my God, are the wonders which You have done, and Your thoughts toward us; There is none to compare with You. If I would declare and speak of them, they would be too numerous to count," Psalms 40:5. It is so comforting and hope-giving to know what God thinks of you and you are on his mind.

Perhaps the old thought patterns have become so much a part of you, so much of a knee jerk reaction. The old thought patterns that diminish your hope and cut up your peace are what is called a "stronghold" in the Bible. A stronghold is something that is developed over time and becomes a repetitive behavior. The *Cambridge English Dictionary* defines strongholds as, "a place that is well defended or is a center for particular beliefs or activities." Strongholds often are built from childhood.

As a child, you may not have known the habitual negative thoughts you accepted in your life were not the truth. Or perhaps you did realize these thoughts were not of God but you did not realize you can have control over them. It is very likely that most of your thoughts were not from God. Isaiah 55:9 says, "For as the heavens are higher than the earth, so are My ways higher than your ways and My thoughts than your thoughts."

Learning to embrace God's thoughts and truths is what gives us hope. God longs to give you the mind of Christ so you may have hope and peace. The thoughts of God are ours if we simply ask. In 1 Corinthians 2:16, we are told that his thoughts are already ours: "Who has known the mind of the Lord so as to instruct him? But we have the mind of Christ."

Appropriating the mind of Christ is about learning to think God-ordained thoughts. Learning to think like Christ takes tenacity. Concentration and mindfulness on God's truth is required to change the predictable or habitual thought patterns that have been developed throughout our lifetimes.

Romans 12:2 says, "Do not conform to the pattern of this world, but be transformed by the renewing of your mind. Then you will be able to test and approve what God's will is—his good, pleasing and perfect will." This verse shows you that when you are transforming your thought patterns to be in line with God's will, hope is the result. When you are proving out in your life God's good, pleasing and perfect will, hope is built in your heart and mind. Your thoughts and beliefs are then reinforced by hope in God's Word and in his love for you.

The tenacity of hope-filled thoughts is realized by the systematic reframing of your thought life. The effort to create thoughts based on God's word, rather than your circumstances, is critical to building and experiencing tenacious hope.

One practical step you can take to establish God's way of thinking is a practice called meditation. Many studies have shown that reading, writing, and speaking out loud helps people to understand and more fully comprehend a new thought or subject. Therefore, it is so important to read, write, meditate on, and speak out God's truths. This tenacious, habit-building practice will replace our faulty thinking with God's thoughts.

Here are some of God's truths (NKJV) you can begin to utilize to meditate on and replace the enemy's lies:

Psalm 139:17: *"How precious also are Your thoughts to me, O God! How vast is the sum of them!"*

Amos 4:13: *"For behold, He who forms mountains and creates the wind and declares to man what are His thoughts, He who makes dawn into darkness and treads on the high places of the earth, the Lord God of hosts is His name."*

Psalm 40:5: *"Many, O Lord my God, are the wonders which You have done, and Your thoughts toward us; There is none to compare with You. If I would declare and speak of them, they would be too numerous to count."*

Matthew 21:22: *"If you believe, you will receive whatever you ask for in prayer."*

Reflect and Respond

What are some thoughts you can identify that are causing you to lose hope? (Hint: what do you say to yourself when no one is around?)

_____

_____

_____

What does God's Word say about those thoughts?

_____

_____

_____

What promises does God's Word have for you regarding a false belief that is attacking your hope?

_____

_____

_____

Jayne Poli serves as Lifeteams Pastor at her church and is passionate about expanding God's Kingdom through creating and training teams, providing a way for people to connect and use their gifts. She has been a pastor's wife for over 30 years and loves serving in the local church. Jayne also enjoys painting, reading, and spending time with family.

18

Tenacious Hope Is Greater Than
What's Before Me

KRISTEN LARSON

"The godly people in the land are my true heroes! I take pleasure in them!"
Psalm 16:3 (NLT)

The people that inspire me toward hope are those who hang onto Jesus through every trying circumstance in their lives. From the outside looking in, it almost feels like their faith comes easily. But I know, in the background, there is a struggle going on. Even people with rock solid faith experience fear. How do I know this? Because I've lived it.

Christmas 2017 started a terrible season of life for me. Over our Christmas vacation, my husband and I were in a head-on collision that totaled our truck. I had to have my wisdom teeth removed. And the worst part—my dad's health plummeted. While the truck issue was resolved for the better and my surgery went smoothly, my dad's health concerns rattled me. His symptoms were such that it took weeks for the doctors to figure out what was going on. There were nights we thought we'd lose him before a diagnosis came. When it finally did, I was both relieved and shocked—relieved because we finally had an answer, but shocked because the answer was lymphoma. Cancer.

Hope is like a muscle. You start out with a small amount of weight and work your way up. Liken it to the person you trust the most: You didn't start out trusting them, but through a series of events, over years or decades, you learned that you could. It took working through circumstances together, learning to compromise, as well as giving and taking for you to trust them as you do now.

What may have put a strain on your relationship *years* ago, you wouldn't bat an eye at now. That muscle is strong and growing stronger every day.

Second Corinthians 4:7-8 (NLT) explains this process well: "We now have this light shining in our hearts, but we ourselves are like fragile clay jars containing this great treasure. This makes it clear that our great power is from God, not from ourselves. We are pressed on every side by troubles, but we are not crushed. We are perplexed, but not driven to despair. We are hunted down, but never abandoned by God. We get knocked down, but we are not destroyed. Through suffering, our bodies continue to share in the death of Jesus so that the life of Jesus may also be seen in our bodies."

My faith heroes had to learn the hard way, too. They had to build that relationship with Jesus through trials and triumphs. But that is all the more reason I call them my heroes and rejoice in them! It's because of their tenacious hope and trust in God that they've become mighty and can now stand amidst the fiercest of storms.

After learning of my dad's diagnosis, I would cry on my way into work while clenching one of my fists—symbolically holding onto Jesus' hand for dear life. I had one hand on the wheel while the other hand white-knuckled Jesus' as I grieved what might be. At night I would join hands with my husband and pray over my parents, recalling what I've learned from the scriptures of God's character, reminding him of what he's done in the past, and declaring that there was more to this story than met the eye. I learned that what happens to my dad affects more than just him, more than just me. I saw how people came forward to support my mom and dad and how many lives were touched by *one* person. My dad's diagnosis did something I never expected: it showed me that I can trust Jesus with my dad's life. And if I can trust him with my dad's life, what *can't* I trust him with?

Tenacious hope isn't something you simply have. It's a decision to seek Jesus first in all things and to learn lessons of faith every single day. It's giving Jesus a chance to work and putting all your eggs in HIS basket.

In whatever circumstances you find yourself, cling to hope and take that first— or hundredth— step. When you get knocked down, get back up again. When fear overwhelms you, squeeze his hand until you have nothing left. He can handle it.

Reflect and Respond

Who are your faith heroes?

_____

_____

_____

How have the challenges you've faced strengthened or diminished your faith?

_____

_____

_____

What might be holding you back from completely placing your hope in Jesus?

_____

_____

_____

Kristen Larson started writing in 2011. Since then she has contributed to Faith Radio Network's blog, written devotionals for Barbour Publishing, and started her dream job working at Bethany House Publishers in Minnesota. To find her online devotional, visit AbideTrustBelieve.wordpress.com.

19

Tenacious Hope Is Greater Than the Darkest Night

CRYSTAL DILL

"For once you were full of darkness, but now you have light from the Lord.
So live as people of light! . . . For the light makes everything visible . . .
This is why it is said, 'Awake, O sleeper, rise up from the dead
and Christ will give you light.'"

Ephesians 5:8, 14 (NLT)

Have you ever felt hopeless in your circumstances?

Maybe you weren't sure where your next pack of diapers was coming from. You didn't know if you would have a home to live in tomorrow. Maybe the hope of your marriage surviving another season was dwindling. Perhaps you or a loved one encountered a dire health situation.

I have experienced and understand the true hopeless feelings that accompany these circumstances.

But circumstances are subject to change when God is involved.

I knew God had a plan. It just felt scary because I hadn't a clue what that plan entailed.

When my husband and I weren't sure how we would afford diapers for our son for the next week, what else was left to do except cry, pray, and hope that somehow God would come through?

The morning we had our moving truck packed and suddenly everything fell through, the emotions I felt were heavy. Rejection, fear, failure, hopelessness.

When my marriage was feeling shaky and I was overcome with a sense of defeat, the thought that there was no hope became overwhelming. Some well-meaning people consoled me in a way that coddled the fear and lies surrounding me, which only drove me further away from the truth.

My faith was further shaken when my friend's brother was diagnosed with a terminal disease. After months of fervent prayer and believing for his miraculous healing, he passed away. The emotions that accompanied that season of our lives included defeat and grief. We knew that he was with Jesus, but we had all been hoping for a different outcome.

Through all these trying circumstances, there were glimmers of hope, but I needed to learn how to position myself in order to get a good view of those gleams.

There is a rock of hope that goes beyond optimism and expectation. There is a rock that is secure. A hope that knows. This rock of hope is greater than any dark night we might face. This hope is Jesus Christ. He is our surest hope.

Romans 13:12 (AMP) says, "The night (this present evil age) is almost gone and the day (of Christ's return) is almost here. So let us fling away the works of darkness and put on the full armor of light."

When we face the most difficult of circumstances, may we remember that we are now children of light. As we sturdy our steps upon Christ, our rock, we will be set like a city on a hill, able to brave the most severe of storms. We will then shine like a beacon of hope for the world to see.

As my husband and I clung to prayer and trusted in who God is, we saw victory unfold in our lives.

The morning we used our last diaper, God led us to church, where someone who wasn't aware of our circumstances gave us enough money to buy diapers.

I'd like to tell you that when our home fell through another one miraculously popped up, but that wasn't the case. Sometimes our prayers aren't answered the way we would like. However, God took care of us along the journey until he brought us to our next place of promise.

After fully surrendering my marriage into God's hands, he began miracles of change, and I'm overjoyed to say we are going on 11 years of marriage in 2018!

Although my prayers for my friend weren't answered in the way I hoped, I know he is with the Lord. My faith was definitely shaken, but now that the dust has settled, the foundation is more firm than ever.

When we allow God room to work through our circumstances, cling to his word and the hope that we have in his plan for our lives, we will surely shine.

The hope we have is needed in the world around us. Let us become beacons of Christ's hope for the world around us to help others get through their own dark nights.

Reflect and Respond

Have any dark nights been looming over your life?

_____

_____

_____

What scriptures can you stand on to remind yourself that you are a child of light?

_____

_____

_____

How can you shine your light to encourage someone else who is experiencing a season of darkness?

_____

_____

_____

Crystal Dill is owner of Double Take, LLC, where she gets to be makeup artist, author, and creative. When she isn't playing with makeup, writing, or speaking, you can find her sharing her heart over a warm cup of coffee or creating her Handmade Halos—a line of greeting cards. More than anything, Crystal enjoys time with Jesus, her husband James, son Lincoln, and their dog, Red. You can find Crystal online at doubletakemn. com.

20

Tenacious Hope is Greater Than My Comfort

KENDRA ROEHL

"Sing to the Lord, all the earth;
proclaim his salvation day after day.
Declare his glory among the nations,
his marvelous deeds among all peoples."

1 Chronicles 16:23-24 (NLT)

I hate to admit it, but I have a strong aversion—dare I say, even loathing—of bugs and snakes, especially those unfamiliar to me.

So when my husband recently approached me about considering another missions trip, this time with all our children, my first thought was, "Yeah, but *where?*" Not because I'm afraid of hard work or humid weather—I'm fine sleeping on a floor and being a little dirty—but whether or not it's likely that I will encounter critters that will freak me out.

Like the time I saw cockroaches in Panama and spiders the size of my hand. (Okay, they *appeared* to be the size of my hand. That may be a slight overstatement.)

Or in Mexico, when we went to invite people to our small church gathering and encountered streets filled with wandering dogs that followed us intently down the dirt roads, growling intermittently.

All memories I'd just as soon forget.

And although I know everyone has their hang-ups or reasons why missions trips are hard for them, the truth is that we all have something to overcome in order to say yes to a new venture.

And that, my friends, is where hope walks through the door. Because hope is what gives me the courage to do what I would otherwise choose *not* to do. Hope reminds me why we go, why we serve, and why we love.

When I focus on the why, the fact that I hate bugs fades into the background.

Because when you've heard another's hard story, when you've shared a meal, shed tears, or connected with someone on a deep level despite language or cultural barriers, and when you know that God's very spirit is in your midst— nothing else matters.

Hope says *go*. Hope says *have courage*. Hope says *listen to another's pain and don't be afraid to enter into it*. Hope says *love well*.

And when I listen to hope, not my fears, I find peace and joy. It may sound impossible, but it's there—right on the other side of the unknown.

I want nothing more for my life than to be one who followed hard after hope, even to the places that I most fear, whether that's in my own neighborhood or halfway around the world.

And although I may also hope that I won't come across any more creepy crawlers, I won't let that stop me from following where God leads me.

Reflect and Respond

What holds you back from saying yes to things that scare you, such as a missions trip?

_____

_____

_____

How can you begin to serve others—in your own community, country, and around the world?

_____

_____

_____

Kendra Roehl is described by her father as a "defender of the weak" and is always looking for those who fall through the gaps and are in need of help. Her natural inclination toward the hurting segued into a career as a clinical social worker, a foster and adoptive mom, and now a writer and speaker. Her most recent book, *The One Year Daily Acts of Kindness Devotional*, can be found wherever books are sold. Connect with her at theruthexperience.com.

21

Tenacious Hope Is Greater Than
My Works

DAWN ZIMMERMAN

"Be still, and know that I am God."
Psalm 46:10 (NLT)

It all started with a friend asking if we could be weekly prayer partners during the Christmas season, as a way to intentionally be present in the season and explore where God wanted to take each of us in the coming year.

It was still November and I had yet to fully feel the expedited pace of the holiday season. But I knew it was coming. A Sunday night check-in sounded simple and would be an opportunity to hear from a friend I loved during a season I loved.

So, I said yes.

Two seconds later, she texted, "Send a me a few things that are on your heart."

My heart. Hmm. Before giving it much thought, I responded that I wanted God to help me set clear professional goals for the new year. What should I be taking on? What should I be letting go of?

While the words did not seem different than any other year, I felt different as I sent them. I want to live a life worthy of his call—and I know that takes intention and reflection.

Over the next week, the word "reset" was on my heart and I asked her to pray about it. I had been known to live at a high-performing pace—for work, for my family, for my friends, for my neighbors, for my community. It didn't matter if

I had a daunting to-do list, I would still try to find a way to meet a request that popped up, too. I wanted God to use me and not waste the time he has given me sitting around. The words of Colossians 3:23 were my mantra, "Whatever you do, do it with all your heart, as working for the Lord." My energy felt unshakable.

Two weeks later, I woke up with intense, unrelenting abdominal pain, barely able to move for an hour. For the first time, I took off several days from work, not even opening my computer. All I had the energy to do was rest—and watch a marathon of Hallmark Christmas movies.

While praying in December, I had imagined that God's "reset" may bring a "new call" for me. I was excited and open to whatever his "next project" was for me. I totally failed to recognize that when we hit reset on something, a shutdown follows. And it's in those quiet moments that the defining work happens.

So often we want to rush the reset. God shut down my body and forced me to learn to do something that I was awful at—resting. How could God use my rest? I felt guilty, like I was wasting time. I was eager to get going again.

We can put rest in a box, as something we do on vacation or Sundays. We can define it too narrowly to sleeping, sitting, or a specific period of time. God's view is bigger and so much more purposeful.

My reboot took what felt like forever—literally months of low energy and operating at what felt like a snail speed. It led me to pull back on my work professionally, at church, and in the community. In that, God taught me a powerful lesson: He actually doesn't need me. He can do it on his own—or choose to equip others. The words of Psalm 46:10 struck me, "Be still, and know that I am God."

Humbled in a new way, I became so grateful. Grateful that he is bigger and not limited in his resources. Grateful for the freedom to not feel like I have to do it all to be worthy of his call. Grateful that he calls us to rest—just like he did on the seventh day of creation. God worked and called it good and then he rested and called it holy.

Our rest is holy. God uses it to refuel, refocus, and refine us. He uses it to remind us that while he appreciates our hustle to do good in his name and for his glory, he's got this. We can rest just as well as we work.

Reflect and Respond

What is God teaching you in your quiet moments?

_____

_____

_____

How can you live out God's model for work and rest?

_____

_____

_____

Dawn Zimmerman is an author, speaker, and trainer who helps organizations shape and share their stories in meaningful ways. But her favorite roles are being Mrs. Zimmerman and "mom" to two kids who teach her every day to seek joy and live in the moment. She's a lover of lakes, adventures, and the unexpected.

SECTION 3

Tenacious
HOPE

Inspires Me To...

22

𝒯enacious 𝒽ope 𝒥nspires 𝓂e 𝒯o
Dance on My Disappointments

AMBER GERSTMANN

"I pray that the eyes of your heart may be enlightened in order that you may know the hope to which he has called you, the riches of his glorious inheritance in his holy people, and his incomparably great power for us who believe.

That power is the same as the mighty strength he exerted when he raised Christ from the dead and seated him at his right hand in the heavenly realms."

Ephesians 1:18-20 (NIV)

In 1849, one wide-eyed ambitious young man left everything and everyone he knew in his cozy Ireland town and set sail for the Americas with vision in his heart and a dream to pursue. James McCabe traveled alone. He was fourteen. He was headed for a Wisconsin homestead and a new life. But somewhere in the journey across the great Atlantic he was shipwrecked and spent three grueling days and nights on the cold rocky banks of Newfoundland, fortunate to be alive, starving, and no doubt afraid, until a passing ship rescued him and brought him to the nearby bustling city of St. John.

James had lost everything.

Imagine the courage it would take to set out at such a young age to pursue that which is in your heart. Then imagine the shock and devastation of coming so close, only to dramatically lose what little remains of your life. How dejected

James must have felt as he took up available work on a farm in Toronto and put off that dream for one more year, one more year, one more year.

But James was one tenacious young man. He developed some grit. He kept his chin up. And he must have chosen to follow hope instead of heartache, for seven years later, James had acquired enough in Toronto to realize his dream. At twenty-one, he moved to Wisconsin and finally purchased his homestead.

James McCabe was my great-great-grandfather. I first heard his story in the midst of a difficult season wherein I felt my own dreams were shipwrecked, and I do not believe for a minute that was coincidental. Tenacious hope is contagious hope. His story makes me want to dance a jig on my own disappointments.

I wonder if tenacity and hopeful optimism are in my bloodline (the jig certainly is!). If genetics have anything to say about making it through to the other side, then perhaps I can claim some advantage. I don't think it works that way though. We are not necessarily genetically wired to hang on in faith through adversity, but we *are* spiritually wired that way.

Tenacious hope *is* in the bloodline, for the same power that raised Christ from the grave lives inside us (Romans 8:11, Ephesians 1:18-20). As daughters who put our hope in Jesus, we are equipped and empowered by him to endure, to succeed, to overcome!

What are you struggling through today? What setback has you reeling and searching and longing? Have you experienced a shipwreck of the soul and aren't sure how to recover?

Can I offer a life preserver from the shores of my own journey through heartbreak? Lean hard into Jesus, who in every moment can give you "strength for today and bright hope for tomorrow" (Thomas Chisholm, *Great Is Thy Faithfulness*). The hope he gives is both our starting line to victory as well as our necessary companion along the way. And I can promise you that, at some point, hope that began as the slightest of breezes will grow into a billowing wind in your sails. And you, my friend, just might start dancing on your own disappointments.

Reflect and Respond

Whose story of tenacity inspires you?

_____

_____

_____

What can you glean from their experience to boost your courage and trust in Jesus for the journey?

_____

_____

_____

Amber Gerstmann is wife to Trevor and momma of three. She's a worship leader, Bible/theology teacher, runner, coffee snob, and foodie. Amber loves to geek out on all things music and theology. One can typically find her chasing her littles, dabbling in photography, or singing (loudly) at the piano.

23

Tenacious Hope Inspires Me To Take Action

KELLY RADI

"Whatever you do, work heartily, as for the Lord and not for men, knowing that from the Lord you will receive the inheritance as your reward. You are serving the Lord Christ."

Colossians 3:23-24 (ESV)

My cousin Becca, one of the most hard-working, successful, faith-filled women I know, has a cute little red sign hanging in her house that says, *"Dreams don't work unless you do."*

She says this sign motivates her to focus on her goals and put the necessary effort into achieving them. It encourages her to be prayerful and action-oriented.

Prayers, like dreams, require us to take action—not to sit idly by and wish. When you pray, you are opening your heart and mind, connecting with the most holy Father, not casting wishes to some sparkly fairy godmother.

As an author, I'd love to just send up a prayer that my book will sell a million copies and then sit back and watch them fly off the shelves. But that's not how it works. I actually have to do the work—research, development, marketing, sales—every day. It takes commitment and grit. I pray for God's guidance on how I can leverage my time and best connect with my audience. I ask him to help me empower other women and honor him in my professional contacts.

Praying from a place of servanthood means asking the all-knowing savior for direction and then following though. This kind of prayer requires tenacious hope.

Does this mean we can still pray for things that seem out of our control? Absolutely! (Philippians 4:6-7). We can drop to our knees and beg for peace and healing and mercy. We are instructed to cast our anxieties on him. But we also need to ask his counsel for our words and actions. Prayer is not an excuse for inaction. In fact, the Bible has a lot to say about taking action.

*"Be **doers** of the Word, and not hearers only, deceiving yourselves." James 1:22*

*"But the one who looks into the perfect law, the law of liberty, and perseveres, being no hearer who forgets but **a doer who acts**, he will be blessed in his **doing**." James 1:23-25*

*"Whatever you **do** in word or deed, do all in the name of the Lord Jesus, giving thanks through Him to God the Father." Colossians 3:17*

*"And let us not grow weary of **doing** good, for in due season we will reap, if we do not give up. So then, as we have opportunity, let us **do good to everyone**, and especially to those who are of the household of faith." Galatians 6:9-10*

Taking action may mean different things to different people. It may mean nurturing a relationship or ending an unhealthy one. It may mean taking a calculated business risk or choosing a new career path. It may mean revising a diet or adding daily physical activity. It may mean giving your time as a volunteer. It may mean humbly praying for a coworker, boss, or relative you don't like very much. It may be actively helping someone else achieve their dreams.

Becca actively helped me when I decided to take a leap of faith and quit my job to start my speaking and writing business. She validated my commitment to honor God through my work. She encouraged me with phone calls, notes, and words of affirmation. She prayed with me and over me. She listened patiently as I shared my fears and counseled me through challenges. And today she is my biggest cheerleader, celebrating my successes and pushing me to work harder and be better. Likewise, I am hers.

As women, we need a certain amount of perseverance and determination to find success in our personal and professional lives. We also need to surround ourselves with other believers who remind us of our essential purpose, who push us to take action, and who dance around the room with us when we have something to celebrate!

Regardless of your career or calling, marital status or age, setting goals that honor the Lord can help you find the success you are seeking. When you step out with tenacious hope and set goals that restore others, he will reward you. Sisters, we must pray for one another, ask for guidance, and live out our faith through action.

Reflect and Respond

This week, make time to reflect on your life over the past 90 days. Revisit and revise your goals. Praise God for your blessings and successes and ask him for the motivation to be tenacious in the area(s) of your life that need more focus.

What do you need to be tenacious about in order to reach your goals?

_____

_____

_____

What specifically can you do this week to offer grace and encouragement to somebody who needs it?

_____

_____

_____

Kelly Radi is a motivational speaker and award-winning author. Her book, *Out To Sea: A Parents' Survival Guide to the Freshman Voyage*, is a resource for parents as they navigate the high school-to-college transition. Connect with her at raditowrite.com.

24

Tenacious Hope Inspires Me To
Set the Course

JACLYN LOWEEN

"Let us hold unswervingly to the hope we profess,
for he who promised is faithful."

Hebrews 12:23 (NIV)

Approaching the start line, I was bogged down with the weight of extra layers in a futile attempt to stay dry as long as possible. The temps hovered around 36 degrees Fahrenheit. The wind was 26 miles per hour, straight into our faces. The rain was relentlessly steady. This trifecta of less than ideal conditions offered plenty of excuses to give up hope, lower expectations, or hang up the dream of having a "good race" to the finish line.

And yet, when my feet crossed the start line, my head, heart, and body were pointed in one direction. There was no other option than to start the 26.2 mile course from Hopkinon to Boston with hope that the finish line and I would meet regardless of the circumstances. The coming miles would not be covered with ease, but my determination to cover them would not be thwarted. I had trained too hard to let that happen, setting me on course for hope to win!

Training plans for the Boston marathon are no joke. Literally, hundreds of miles had been run in preparation for this race. What I didn't realize about my training (until it was put to the test on one of the worst combinations of race conditions) is that it would provide me with not just the physical strength to endure, but the emotional, mental, and spiritual muscles to run with confident hope toward a finish line I knew was there waiting for me.

As I ran, gusts of wind swayed my body every so slightly, while the rain penetrated every centimeter of my clothing. My feet sloshed around in my shoes. Attempting some reprieve, I would tuck behind other runners whenever possible. All of this should have discouraged me, slowed me down, and given me permission to take it easy.

But that wasn't what happened. Instead, grace, strength, hope, and my clarity of purpose became stronger. My focus on the finish line that day was sharper and more consistent than any other race I have run. It was as if the daunting circumstances pressing against me from the left and the right steadied my eyes and determination to only be able to point forward. There was no room for distractions.

I had to rely on my training to get me through. I had to believe that because my body had run 26.2 miles before, it could do it again. I had to believe that my muscles knew what to do and would take me there if my mind let them. My mantra from mile 22 on was, "Let your legs carry you in. They know what to do. Let your legs carry you in." I had a choice to make with each mile: To trust in the hope that I could make it to the finish line with the strength gained in training, or believe the lie that I couldn't.

What I discovered is that it actually was hard to believe the lie because there were so many memories in my mind of finishing strong. My training miles and races from the past had built into my brain as evidence to support the truth of who I am, what I can endure, and what I can accomplish. Because of the courses my muscles and mind had experienced in the past, there was only room for hope, confidence, and truth.

But life is full of courses that put our soul, heart, and mind to the test. When we sign up for the Christian race of faith, we get to submit to the training plans outlined for us in the Bible.

And we start running. Some days are "easy" training days. Other days are slow and long. And some days feel like we're racing into the wind and the rain. What gets us through those really hard days?

I believe it is setting the course for hope to win by training your soul, heart, and mind to believe you have what it takes to run the race marked out for you (Hebrews 12). This isn't a one-time activity you check off a list. Instead, it is built on season after season of choosing to train your soul, heart, and mind to know, believe, and live out the commands and truths (training plan) recorded in the Bible.

For example, taking every thought captive and turning it over to the obedience of Christ (2 Corinthians 10:5) becomes a habit that trains your soul, heart, and mind toward hope. The more you train your mind in this manner, the stronger your spiritual muscles grow and the greater confidence you have in the hope you profess because you have memories (evidence) that supports the truth.

My physical training has had an amazing and powerful impact on my spiritual journey. I find that when I train my body to endure challenging circumstances, I learn how to apply those same tactics to fighting for faith, hope, and truth to win. Setting the course for hope to win against doubt and giving up begins with submitting to the training plans provided in Scripture. Then, choosing to run courses that require you to use confident hope to run toward God's purposes and plans for now and eternity. Finally, it's believing there is a finish line, and that you are designed to run full-on toward it.

Reflect and Respond

What would it look like to choose to submit to a training plan that builds your strength to "run your race" with confident hope toward the finish line of heaven?

_____

_____

_____

Take a few minutes and make a list of all the times God has given you the strength to overcome hardships. Post this on your mirror, fridge, or kitchen sink window to remind you that your hope is being built every day, providing evidence to boost your confidence to endure the race ahead.

_____

_____

_____

Jaclyn Loween is a daughter, sister, friend, wife, mom, teacher, runner, and blogger at jaclynloween.com. Her desire is to help others know who they are in Christ and how to run confidently in life and faith.

25

Tenacious Hope Inspires Me To Act in Faith and Joy

SUE MOORE DONALDSON

"May the God of hope fill you with all joy and peace as you trust in him, so that you may overflow with hope by the power of the Holy Spirit."

Romans 15:13 (NIV)

In my late 20s, I was home visiting my folks a few days. Mom had just returned from her Women's Bible Study. She walked in the living room, put down her purse and exclaimed: "Sue, I just studied about the children of Israel, who were told to step down into the Jordan River and that *then* the water would rise up on either side. So I've decided to open a savings account for you—for your wedding!"

"Uh, Mom, I'm not even dating."

"That doesn't matter. God told those people to step out in faith first, and *then* the water would disappear and they would be able to walk to the other side. So I'll begin saving today in faith, believing in hope that you will someday get married!"

Poor Mom. The last of her five kids hadn't closed the deal yet, and she was worried. I was too, at times, and hoped that someday my prince would come. I hadn't started a savings account, however.

Did Mom have the right idea? Are we supposed to act on our faith, believing in hope that God will answer our prayers? I can't answer that question for all your prayers, nor for all my prayers. I just know that she knew God was speaking to her through an ancient text, and she acted on it in faith and joy.

"Now the Jordan is at flood stage all during harvest. Yet as soon as the priests who carried the ark reached the Jordan and their feet touched the water's edge, the water from upstream stopped flowing," Joshua 3:15,16 (NIV).

I remembered that story recently while praying for my daughter's boyfriend to come to know Jesus. We love Jeff. We've known him over three years. He's gone to church with us, he loves our daughter, he thinks we're fanatics (I assured him we are!), and he still hangs around whenever he can. While bringing him and his doubting heart to Jesus that day, I suddenly thought: "Okay, then. In faith believing, I'm going to start saving money for Jeff's 'Salvation Celebration!'"

Jeff is a foodie. He likes an expensive dinner out, including appetizers and dessert. I can't really afford the kind of party Jeff would appreciate. But God can. I got up from my prayer chair, reached for a crystal vase, and stuffed in all my loose change and a five-dollar bill.

"There," I thought. "I'm just like Mom. I'm going to keep filling this vase on faith that God will answer our prayers for a lost lamb who needs to come home."

I've been stuffing bills and pouring change into that vase for close to a year now. I can buy dinner for one person—maybe two—but the vase isn't full yet. I pray daily in hope, believing that Jeff will repent, acknowledge his need of a Savior, and start the relationship he was created for.

It hasn't happened yet.

There are days I feel discouraged. But then I look up at the top of the china cabinet and see a bunch of money in a crystal vase and ask God one more time:

Lord, this is your desire—that all men come to yourself. I'm not telling you when or how, but I am asking you, by faith and hope believing, to save this young man. Amen.

And then I scrounge through my purse, find some change and plop it in the vase.

Tenacious faith includes action. Sometimes that action involves money, and sometimes it looks foolish. Sometimes it's a little bit of both. But the more I save, the greater my resolve to keep knocking on God's door for the sake of Jeff's eternity. I'm expecting quite a party, and I hope it happens by the time you read this.

As for my Mom's savings account, when I finally got engaged almost ten years after her grand action of faith and hope, she commented on how much my bridal dress cost. I queried, "Well, what about the savings account, Mom?"

"I spent it!" she replied.

Ha! I guess a mother's faith can only take so much. I loved my Mom for starting it anyway.

And she still paid for the dress.

Reflect and Respond

What do you need more faith for right now? Do you need to do something to put "feet to your faith"?

_____

_____

_____

Where is God asking you to act in faith and joy, believing in hope for what you are praying for? (It may involve a new savings account. Try not to spend it!)

_____

_____

_____

Sue Moore Donaldson speaks and writes to introduce God's welcoming heart—inviting you to know the Ultimate Host and pass on his invitation. She and her husband Mark live on the Central Coast of California and have raised three semi-adult daughters (which means she's always at the bank or on her knees). Sue blogs at welcomeheart.com/sue-donaldson, and is a frequent speaker for women's events. You may view speaking topics at: welcomeheart.com/speaking.

26

Tenacious Hope Inspires Me To
be an Aged Blue Cheese

SONJA BINDERT

"And let us run with perseverance the race marked out for us, fixing our eyes on Jesus, the pioneer and perfecter of faith. For the joy set before him he endured the cross, scorning its shame, and sat down at the right hand of the throne of God. Consider him who endured such opposition from sinners, so that you will not grow weary and lose heart."

Hebrews 12:1-3 (NIV)

Yes, you read the title correctly; I did say I wanted to be an aged blue cheese. You see, on my fortieth birthday this year, I joked with my husband that I had become "old and moldy." With a facetious grin he kindly responded, "You know, I always thought my wife would age like a fine wine. Instead, she is aging like a fine blue cheese!" We shared a much needed laugh, a laugh that expressed joy despite the year we had endured, having just received my diagnosis of chronic inflammatory response syndrome. In other words, I was full of mold toxins because my DNA is incapable of creating antibodies to rid itself of these mycotoxins, causing a cascade of inflammatory responses.

You may wonder how there could be joy in the midst of this diagnosis, but for a year I had had thirty different symptoms that made me sick and fatigued. Seven months prior to my diagnosis, I had gone to the ER with blurred vision, difficulty finding words, numbness, and tingling that spread through the right side of my body and face. An MRI of my brain showed multiple lesions, leaving the neurologist asking why my brain looked like that of a 60-year-old. Was it Lyme's, multiple sclerosis, or another autoimmune disease? I endured more testing without any answers, leaving me asking, "Am I crazy? Am I making this stuff up?"

As a blue cheese is ripening to perfection, it undergoes "needling" which allows air to feed the penicillium culture that will develop into the blue-veined, velvety cheese that only a refined palate can truly appreciate. Having finally received a diagnosis, I didn't have to undergo any more needling. It had been determined that I had mold of the stachybotrys variety thriving in my veins, but unlike the aged blue cheese, my mold cultivated acne, weight gain, a swollen face, fatigue, and a person whose body couldn't cook dinner for her family on many occasions. Definitely not refined . . . or was I?

During this season of the unknown, I had feelings of anger, depression, fear, and happiness, but I found that I had a constant undercurrent of joy running through my entire life, no matter what I faced. My motto was, "I'm glad Jesus loves me enough to refine me."

How is it that I had joy even when I was angry and fearful? It's during this time that I learned the gift of joy from the Holy Spirit does not only show itself as a feeling but as a perception—God's perception—which gives us a true perspective on our circumstances.

I had days that I felt guilty for not being "disciplined" enough. I couldn't focus on reading my Bible or devotionals due to the mold invading my brain. My emotions were running rampant, causing internal conflict. One day, during an emotional let-down with a friend, she reminded me, "This is why you hide God's word in your heart, for times like this when you're caught in a storm and unable to focus." She was right!

When fear of the unknown tried to settle in, the truth from Deuteronomy 31:8 (NIV) resounded through my mind, providing a tenacious hope: "The Lord himself goes before you and will be with you; he will never leave you nor forsake you. Do not be afraid; do not be discouraged."

When I questioned my future and the future of my family, the Holy Spirit reminded me, "I know the plans I have for you, plans to prosper you and not harm you, plans to give you hope and a future," Jeremiah 29:11 (NIV).

And when the devil tried to make me feel like the battle was lost, I remembered the cross, that no matter what happens in this life, we will get the last laugh in heaven because of what Jesus did for us when he defeated the devil and all his schemes once and for all.

If we are to be holy like Jesus, know that Jesus had his father's perception, which gave him a true perspective that brought him joy when he died on the cross for you. "For the joy set before him, he endured the cross, scorning its shame, and sat down at the right hand of the throne of God," Hebrews 12:2 (NIV). Jesus had an undercurrent of joy when he went to the cross, knowing that his sacrifice meant eternity with you and our Father!

So whether you are a young wine, a fine, aged wine, or an aged blue cheese like me—their characteristic flavors come from the air slowly penetrating their exteriors, just as our refinement and character comes from the very breath of God slowly penetrating our hearts and minds during the most challenging seasons of our lives. Embrace the refinement that comes through hardship, as it aligns your heart with God's. View all situations through God's Word, apply God's perspective to all situations, and let his truth be your undercurrent of joy so that you will not grow weary and lose heart but will thrive with a tenacious hope!

Reflect and Respond

Don't deny your natural feelings; to do so would be to deny your humanity. Simply identify your feelings and look at them through the lens of Jesus' perspective. What lies have you listened to that made you feel less than or unable to run the race of life with joy?

_____

_____

_____

What godly truths can replace those lies or feelings and change your perception of life's hardships, allowing you to embrace a tenacious hope? What truths will empower you and provide joy in the midst of anger, fear, depression, numbness, unhappiness, or any of life's difficult situations?

_____

_____

_____

Sonja Bindert is a wife, homeschooling mama of two beautiful girls, and advisor for Bridging the Gap, where she manages The Bridge Shop, a nonprofit that raises money for missions and anti-human trafficking efforts. She loves living life with Jesus because "His plans are so much better than mine!"

27

Tenacious Hope Inspires Me to
Try Again

JANAE LENNING

"Yes, and I will continue to rejoice, for I know that through your prayers and God's provision of the Spirit of Jesus Christ what has happened to me will turn out for my deliverance. I eagerly expect and hope that I will in no way be ashamed, but will have sufficient courage so that now, as always, Christ will be exalted in body, whether by life or by death."

Philippians 1:18-20 (NIV)

My first winter of high school was marked by a ski accident, which coincidentally was followed almost exactly one year later by a bad car accident. Maybe it's poor luck, maybe it's just the game of probability, or maybe it's a consistent reminder—via chronic pain—that the earth we inhabit is broken. Maybe it's all three. Whatever the reason for these unhappy events, despair has been one of the long-lasting results.

At first, when tragedy strikes our lives and burns a dream to the ground, hope may still appear to be living within the embers. But what about when every treatment, medication, therapy, or solution fails you? I've tried everything from physical therapy to acupuncture, epidurals to various medications. I've even tried essential oils placed in my belly button. Years of failed attempts have worked against hope, whispering to me that all I can expect from the future is pain, heartache, and loss.

Do you ever feel this way? That the whole world is out to get you or that God has chosen to walk away from you rather than coming close with his holy comfort? I certainly have.

And so, this is where I choose to say enough is enough to despair, the arch nemesis of hope. Our spiritual reality, which we claim as transcendent truth, is found in the resurrection of Jesus, the authority of Scripture, the presence of the Spirit, and the true love of the Father. Despair may temporarily reign in this world, the way it did on Good Friday. Darkness feels much more victorious than any of us would like. But—there is always a "but"—we can choose to look toward the hope of the future we have been given. Our inheritance as beloved children of God is that things will not always be this way. The state of affairs at the present time is only temporary! When every battle pushes us further and further away from the hope of the Gospel, we must run back to it with everything we have. Because our life is found with Christ on high, we can continually rejoice in knowing what is to come for ourselves and for our world.

We know that in the end, good triumphs over evil. We know that our God will bring us out of pain and into paradise. We know that Christ will be exalted above all, in everything.

Yet, if I'm being honest with you, sometimes this truth feels like a theoretical idea with few real-life implications. So what do we do right now, when pain has overwhelmed our hearts? Our eternally powerful hope can inspire us to try again. Yes, we've taken hits from this broken world, but it's time for us to try again for deliverance—even if it's one step at a time.

Oh, I know in a weary state, letting in even the smallest amount of hope for change is like summiting a mountain. Fatigue of the spirit feels unsurmountable. This is when I pray for the same power that raised Jesus from the grave to get my heart up off the couch and into the throne room. Our precious, beautiful Jesus is the reminder that Sunday morning comes, the captive is set free, and all traces of sadness are gently erased in the light of glorious hope.

The only way out of this is forward, my friend. Whatever struggle you're facing, our Lord is faithfully on the journey with you. I pray that today would be the first step into your hope-filled future, where you courageously try again to fight for the restoration we are promised in Jesus' name.

Reflect and Respond

Where has despair taken root, keeping you waving that white flag instead of readying for battle?

_____

_____

_____

What is one small step you can take today to move toward a future of hope?

_____

_____

_____

Janae Lenning is a recent Wheaton College grad who taught English in France for the past year before coming back to the USA in preparation for the next big adventure abroad. Since the age of 14 she's dealt with fibromyalgia but fights back with real truth, laughter, and the joy of her Savior.

28

Tenacious Hope Inspires Me To
Be Brave

MOLLIE JOY RUSHMEYER

"This is my command—be strong and courageous!
Do not be afraid or discouraged.
For the Lord your God is with you wherever you go."

Joshua 1:9 (NLT)

Cold sweat prickled against my neck. My body, from head to heel, shook with fear. Blinking back tears, I gripped the operating table as pain and pressure collided where the cardiologist dug into a vein in my leg. He worked quietly, inserting the disk that would hopefully cover a hole in my heart and prevent a second stroke—the first of which had come just over a month before.

A deluge of thoughts, fears, and doubts poured over me in great rushing tides. Crashed against my fragile hold on hope, my brittle faith.

What if the goodbyes I said this morning were my last? My children need me, God. Do you hear me? My husband needs me. I'm not ready to die. Yeah, glory and all that. But I'm not ready. And do I really trust this little disk in my heart to be all that lies between my health and another devastating stroke? Will I recover? What if something worse happens? And, yes, because it's that important, I want to know, will I ever write again? Do you even hear me in this horrid, pain-filled moment? This hurts! So much more than physically. It hurts down to my soul.

But as I lay on that table, not knowing what the future might hold, I breathed deep. I squeezed my eyes shut against the pain. Against the panic squeezing around my ribcage. I went to the quiet, hushed place inside. My brave place.

Over the years, that's where I've always gone when something too agonizing has come along. I'd call it an emotional retreat—not the basking-on-the-sand kind of retreat, more like the wave-a-white-flag retreat. I'd muster up whatever courage and hope I had for something better waiting on the other side and told myself to suck it up. I could handle it. This brave place made me feel strong. I could handle whatever life dished out. I remember thanking God on more than one occasion that this incredible coping mechanism had brought me out of some hard circumstances in my life.

The problem was, this time, it didn't work.

This time, anxiety and depression sucked the hope out of my soul. This time, alone in my brave place, it was just me in the dark, and I couldn't scrape together enough bravery to get through it.

Lord, I can't be brave this time, my heart whispered.

And I felt him say in return, *You don't have to be. I'm right here.*

In that moment, something occurred to me—it was never *my* brave place. It was *his*. In my short-sightedness, peripheral blindness, and continual need to do things on my own, I hadn't turned to see he was right beside me all those times. He brought me through the worst times in my life—not me and my ability to be brave enough.

And now, in this most dire of circumstances, I needed to invite him in, make him Lord of this brave place. Not because he hadn't been there all along but because he desires my humility and a maturing, loving relationship with me.

My courage is the direct outpouring of the strength he gives me and his presence with me. His *love* makes me brave. It makes me tenaciously hopeful for the future, miraculous health and recovery, blessings over my family whom I desperately love, his hand on my passions and dreams, and for a greater intimacy and knowledge of him who calls me child and beloved.

There is no true brave place without him.

We are not only encouraged but commanded to be brave in the face of our trials. Let's just not forget to look to our side where our King stands beside us, ready for battle. And remember the prowling lion, Satan, who seeks to slash away our hope with lies like, *'God doesn't love me because he allowed this painful experience'* or *'He's abandoned me.'* Ask God to surround you with his peace and presence. Ask him to be your brave place and refuge against life's storms today. And then cast your worries upon him, clinging to his truth, love, and reckless, tenacious hope that defies all the enemy and this world can throw at it.

Reflect and Respond

What hardships in your life have you gone through in which you've had to be brave?

_____

_____

_____

Visualize your brave place. What are you surrounded by? Who is with you? What words do you hear as you sit quietly and simply listen?

_____

_____

_____

Mollie Rushmeyer lives in Central Minnesota with her husband and two daughters. As a fiction writer, she brings stories of hope to prodigal gals just like her. She's the vice president of her state's American Christian Fiction Writers chapter, a journalist, and writer for Romance Readers' Café.

29

Tenacious Hope Leads Me to
Live Generously

JULIE FISK

"You are all children of the light and children of the day. We do not belong to the night or to the darkness. But since we belong to the day, let us be sober, putting on faith and love as a breastplate, and the hope of salvation as a helmet. For God did not appoint us to suffer wrath but to receive salvation through our Lord Jesus Christ. He died for us so that, whether we are awake or asleep, we may live together with him. Therefore encourage one another and build each other up, just as in fact you are doing."

1 Thessalonians 5:5, 8-11 (NIV)

Next to my bathroom mirror is a small cork board covered in inspirational quotes and graduation announcements we received this spring. These are the thoughts and young people I see each morning as I brush my teeth and apply my eyeliner, and I dwell on and pray over them as I start and end each day.

One of my favorite slips of paper on that board is a quote by Eleanor Roosevelt: "It is better to light a candle than curse the darkness."

This has been my mantra of late, my mental and physical response to a world filled with fear—a world in which suicide rates are up and school shootings are reoccurring rather than a rarity; a world in which hopelessness seems to permeate the very fabric of our society as we watch stories of earthquakes and volcanoes, war and strife, and unexplainable violence against innocents scroll across our screens.

As a woman who loves Jesus, I am sent to light candles—to carry the tenacious hope of Jesus Christ into the lives of those immediately around me. I am to be a hope-bringer: a woman who pushes back against the darkness with her words and actions; a woman who is intentional about compassionately noticing her neighbors, coworkers, and the people who cross her path; a woman who knows the love of her Savior and is determined to reflect that love onto the people around her.

The question I wrestle with as I read Eleanor's words each morning is this: How do I—an ordinary woman living quietly in the Midwest—push back against the terrible things in my newsfeed? How do I bring hope in the midst of someone else's personal tragedy?

I've found that the Holy Spirit's whispered response is a gently, daily reminder to never underestimate the ability of Christ to use us—and our lives—to bring hope to those around us.

While the Holy Spirit uses us to foster hope in a number of ways, I am learning that practicing generosity—with my time, with my skill sets, with the resources God has placed in my hands—puts me in situations and relationships in which the tenacious hope we have in Jesus is revealed in spectacular fashion. It is in our faith lived out loud that we best demonstrate how deep and wide and big the love of God truly is.

Lest you think otherwise, let me reassure you that the habit of generosity is a journey, a practice learned through trial and error. I fail often, missing opportunities because I was grumpy that afternoon, because I can be oblivious to the obvious, because my own garbage sometimes rises up and chokes out my best intentions. But I do not quit. I ask God for second chances, for a redo, for redemption—and then I try again.

Because our tenacious hope is in knowing that eternal life awaits us, that we have no time to lose with our one wild and precious life, and that we are called to share that truth with as many people as possible.

Let us be women who light candles, women who are called to action, women who practice extravagant generosity in response to the darkness of this world. Let us be hope-bringers.

Reflect and Respond

Who around you needs to be reminded of the extravagant love and hope found in Jesus today?

_____

_____

_____

What small thing can you do to express that love and reveal that hope?

_____

_____

_____

As a challenge, be intentionally generous on a daily basis for the next 20 days to start a new habit.

_____

_____

_____

Julie Fisk is passionate about encouraging women to embrace the calling of God in their everyday lives. She and Aaron strive to love God and love others and are raising their children to do the same. They succeed, fail, and rely upon Christ and his grace to fill in their gaps.

30

Tenacious Hope Inspires Me To
Surrender

DAWNA JOHNSON

*"Trust in the Lord with all your heart,
and do not lean on your own understanding.
In all your ways acknowledge him, and he will make straight your paths."*
Proverbs 3:5-6 (ESV)

Have you ever been asked to ride blindfolded in the backseat of a car, trusting and hoping that you would make it safely to your anticipated destination? It sounds crazy and a bit silly, but this is how I felt about four years ago.

I was on my way to a women's conference when the Lord began to speak to my heart. He asked if I would give him control of my life. I was shocked!

Lord, what do you mean give you control? I thought I did that ages ago?

I could feel the Lord shaking his head, as he revealed what I had failed to realize. Not only was I in the driver's seat, keeping a tight grip on the steering wheel of my life, but I had thrown him in the trunk!

You don't understand, Lord. The desires of my heart are too important to be left to chance! I have to do everything in my power to make things happen in a timely fashion. I mean, c'mon, I have to stay in step with all the successful and accomplished friends I see every day on Facebook!

But in my heart of hearts, I knew he was right. I was messing things up big time. Out of fear, I had spent the past eight years in a job that I had grown to hate.

Not to mention, it was nowhere near the anticipated career I had originally planned for myself. I kept putting off starting a family in order to pursue the career I so desperately desired. Furthermore, I was making choices that worked for me but gave no consideration to how they would affect my husband. I was frustrated, disappointed, and unhappy with my life, and I was too prideful to admit what I knew to be true.

Okay, Lord, where do we go from here?

His answer? Surrender.

Yikes! I believed the Lord had something better than I could ever hope for or imagine, but I wondered if there was any way to get there other than the path he was suggesting.

In this case, the answer was no.

Surrender it is!

This act of surrender began a three-year transformation of my life. I laid down my job. I laid down my body. I laid down the career I had dreamed about since I was a little girl. You name it; I laid it down. I let the Lord do a total reset. As all of these things faded away, I began to see a new hope and future for myself. One that was not defined by my circumstances but by what God was doing in me.

So much of my identity had become wrapped up in what I did and what I wanted that God had to strip it all away so I could see the truth.

The scary part of hopeful surrender, is not knowing what is coming next. I think we would all line up to lay things down if we knew what was going to be on the other side. I can easily get distracted by my desire for the details and fail to see what I do now: That God's best is always on the other side of surrender.

"For I know the plans I have for you, declares the Lord, plans to prosper you and not to harm you, plans to give you a hope and a future," Jeremiah 29:11 (NIV).

I can walk confidently in surrender, because I know without a doubt that God has my best interest at heart. Whether he puts me on a stage performing before thousands or places me at a desk to keep a company organized, I know that my fulfillment and joy comes from the Lord. Time and time again, the Lord had outdone himself with what he has done in my life. All because I let him lead and take control.

Living a life surrendered to Christ is not easy, but if we tenaciously hope in the promises found in his Word, we will not be disappointed!

Reflect and Respond

If God were to examine your life today, who would he find in the driver's seat?

_____

_____

_____

Are there areas in your life that you need to turn over to him?

_____

_____

_____

How can you take one step toward surrender today?

_____

_____

_____

Dawna Johnson is a worship leader, songwriter, and recording artist from Minneapolis, MN. She currently serves as the Worship Director for Wooddale Church at their Loring Park downtown campus. When she is not doing ministry, she spends her time savoring precious moments with her family and friends.

31

Tenacious Hope Inspires Me To
Wonder

KRISTEN OSTREM

"Surely goodness and lovingkindness will follow me all the days of my life..."
Psalm 23:6 (NASB)

While touring Manhattan, New York, my mom and I stopped to inquire about the cost of visiting the 1 World Trade Center (WTC) observation deck. After hearing the price, I immediately decided it was a no-go during this trip to the Big Apple. I didn't want to spend the money and had already had the privilege of seeing the Empire State Building observation deck in middle school.

Despite saying no, my soul had a sparkle of curiosity that whispered, "It would be neat to go up."

We continued walking and found our way to the memorial fountains honoring the hundreds of lives lost on September 11, 2001. Before leaving the area, my mom and I asked each other one final time, "Do you want to go up?"

"Well," I thought, "I don't *need* to go, and I *think* I know what it will be like."

But after considering the options, my mom decided, "Let's do it! It's a piece of our history."

With our decision made, we headed toward the ticketing booth. Who would have known the experience to follow would be one of our favorites during this mother-daughter vacation?

The 1 WTC is the tallest skyscraper in North America, housing some of the fastest elevators in the Western Hemisphere. In line for the elevator, we watched interviews of workers who built the behemoth building, and I was amazed at their bravery. We read structural facts, watched a video of the rooftop spire being lowered into place, and heard testimonials of the tower's symbolism to NYC and America as a whole.

We approached the elevator, and the doors opened. It was our turn. Before we knew it, we were thrust 102 stories upward in just 47 seconds. The ride was an experience of its own! As we rose in altitude, the elevator walls featured a 360-degree video of New York City's rise in development over the past 500 years.

Exiting the elevator, we found ourselves open-mouthed at the sights from the 360-degree, indoor observation deck. We identified the city's boroughs and Hoboken, New Jersey. We saw Hudson Bay, bustling with boats, and the Staten Island Ferries. We witnessed what appeared to be LEGO-sized structures and ant-sized people. The view stretched on for miles, and with so much in between, it was breathtaking!

After returning to ground level, we remained in awe of God's goodness for the rest of the night. He's the one who led us to the wonder-filled experience. It almost felt as though our initial curiosity-twinkle was God's beckoning, wanting to show us something we didn't even *know* we wanted to see.

My mom once gave me a wooden sign that reads, "Always believe something wonderful is about to happen." I love that saying, because it reminds me to hope in *God*—to wonder with expectation what he is going to do with my circumstances.

Whether riding elevators on vacation or riding through the storms of life, we will surely see God's goodness come through, if we're looking for it.

In the 2004 Pixar movie, *The Incredibles*, the protagonist Parr family has superpowers. One day, the neighbor boy, Rusty McAllister, is shown waiting on his trike for Bob Parr (a.k.a. Mr. Incredible) to get home from work. When Bob arrives, he sees the boy sitting in his driveway and begrudgingly asks, "What are you waiting for?"

Rusty replies with exclamation, "I don't know! Something amazing, I guess!"

Even not knowing what might happen, Rusty believed he would see something extraordinary. Like him, do we hope to see the goodness of God throughout our day? Do we believe his lovingkindness will follow us? Are we willing to listen to his still, small voice speaking to us, believing the wisdom he reveals?

Many times, I disregard God's whispers of wisdom, encouragement, or discipline. I can let fear speak louder than truth. Yet, each day we have the the opportunity to look for him again. To hope in him anew. And to have curious wonder for what God will do.

Reflect and Respond

What has God's goodness looked like in your life within the past year or even the past week?

_____

_____

_____

In what ways can you embrace wonder today?

_____

_____

_____

Kristen Ostrem is an adventurer who is growing in the love of God, deeply values her family, is an encourager of the Church, and is grateful for her job with Bridging the Gap.

Made in the USA
Lexington, KY
15 October 2018